Good at English

김 상 한

KNOWLEDGE COMMUNITY 공동체

본 서는 교양 또는 각종의 영어시험을 준비하고자 하는 대학신입생을 위한 초중급의 영어교재이다. 영어에 좀처럼 자신감을 갖지 못하는 학생 대부분은 기초어휘가 부족하고 수준에 맞는 글을 많이 접하지 않은 탓이다. 따라서 일상생활에 흔히 쓰이는 어휘, 문장, 글을 학습할 수 있도록 구성하였다. 여행, 직업, 성격, 외모, 음식, 가정, 동・식물, 여가, 날씨, 건강 등은 토플, 토익 또는 취업영어에 자주 등장하는 주제이기도 하다.

본 서는 "practice makes perfect"(2012)의 후속편이다. 10개의 일상적 주제, 기초어휘 200개와 파생어 및 관련어에 한정하여 영어 학습의 새로운 습관을 목표로 하였다. 먼저 동의어와 반의어를 풍부하게 하자. 어떤 글의 어느 곳에서 취소하다 call off/cancel이 나오면, 다른 곳에 예약하다 book/reserve가 등장하고, 고용하다 hire/employ가 나오면 해고하다 fire/lay off가 보인다. 단어를 익힐 때 believe in/trust, doubt/suspect, happy/satisfied, unhappy/dissatisfied의 방식으로 외자. 둘째로 어휘의 스펙트럼을 만들자. 값싼 cheap, 비싼 expensive를 알면, cheap/reasonable/expensive로 정리하는 것이다. 즉, short/medium height/tall, thin/slim/fit/overweight/fat, single/engaged/married/divorced, warm/hot/chilly/cold 등을 예로 들 수 있다. 이러한 어휘의 스펙트럼은 우리의 표현력을 풍부하게 만들어 준다. 셋째, 짝이 되는 어휘는 함께 기억하자. host and guest, hammer and nail, cup and saucer, back and forth, slow and steady, on and off 등이다. 이처럼 관련어에 익숙하면 그만큼 읽는 속도나 이해가 빨라질 수밖에 없다. 마지막으로 여러 가지 뜻으로 쓰이는 어휘에 유의하자. he <u>stands</u> her rude behavior / she is <u>plain</u> / please <u>season</u> your steaks / I sat on the <u>toilet</u> 등을 제대로 해석할 수 있어야 할 것이다.

짧은 문장을 많이 암기하자. 문장은 짧을수록 이해가 쉽고, 잘 외워진다. 각 Unit은 2개의 부분으로 나뉘어 있고, 각각의 앞부분에 간략한 설명과 더불어 10개씩의 짧은 문장이 열거되어 있다. 수식어가 절제되었으며, 주어/동사가 하나씩 있는 단문이다. 예를 들어, Weather can affect our daily lives *(in a number of ways from our mood to how we go about our day)* 또는 A sanitation worker was injured *(as he was riding on the back of a garbage truck)*. 각 Unit에 ★표 된 20개의 문장은 암기될 때까지 10번 이상 큰 소리로 읽고 써보자.

Preface

무엇보다도 문맥의 파악에 힘쓰자. 모르는 단어가 나오더라도 결코 좌절하지 말자. 예컨대 panic을 모르더라도 'When I saw my son wasn't breathing I panicked, I didn't know what to do.'를 계속 읽으면, 'panic'이란 어쩔 줄 몰라 하는 공황상태임을 짐작할 수 있다. 사전에 의존하기보다는 앞뒤의 문장을 여러 번 읽어 그 뜻을 추정해보면 문제해결력이 생긴다. 이것이야말로 진정한 실력이 아니겠는가?

본 서는 1,270개의 다양한 문제를 수록하고 있다. 대부분은 문맥의 파악에 주력하였으며, 상당수는 어떤 주제와 관련되는 일련의 어휘를 익히며, 일부는 문법적인 내용을 담고 있다. Unit의 본문, [exercise], 〈test〉에서 맞히지 못한 문제는 체크해 두었다가 10번이고, 20번이고 반복 연습하자. 우리는 틀린 유형의 문제를 계속 실수하는 경향이 있기 때문이다. 책의 끝부분에 있는 자기소개 〈Let me introduce myself〉는 나중의 취업인터뷰에 유용할 것이다.

본 서가 독자에게 생활의 새로운 지평을 열 수 있는 기회가 되길 기원한다. 영어학습을 통하여 다른 문화권의 생활스타일, 사상, 지식에 관심과 열정을 키우는 것이야말로 우리의 자산을 풍요롭게 하는 초석임을 믿는다. 아무쪼록 본 서가 제군에게 영어소양과 취업영어의 열쇠가 되길 바란다.

2013년 2월
녹동 서재에서
저자

Contents

Contents

Contents

Unit

01

Travel abroad

Unit. 01 Travel abroad

1 Arrive and depart

다음의 단어 중에서 모르는 것이 있어요?

come, go, book, board, fly, land

이쯤은 '식은 죽 먹기'(a piece of cake)?

오다, 가다, 책, 판자, 파리, 육지

그러나 이들 단어가 모두 동사(verbs)라면? book은 '책/장부' 이외에 장부에 기록하다 즉 '예약하다'의 뜻으로도 쓰인다.

★ Did you **book** a flight and hotel?

board는 '판자/식사/위원회' 이외에 판자에 올라서다 즉 '탑승하다'의 뜻도 있다. 따라서 boarding pass는 탑승권

★ Please **board** the flight.

Show me your **boarding** pass.

fly는 '파리' 이외에 '비행하다,' land는 '육지 /나라' 외에 '착륙하다' 뜻도 있다.

★ I **fly** from Incheon to Beijing.

I **take a** nonstop **flight** to Los Angeles.

★ He knows how to **land** an airplane.

arrive → arrival(도착), depart → departure(출발), come/came/come, go/went/gone, **fly/flew/flown,** some cake; two pieces of cake book(= reserve; make a reservation), booking(= reservation), flight(항공편)

board(= get on), room and board (객실과 식사), board of directors(이사회)

fly(= take a flight), 비행기(an airplane/a plane/ a **flight**/aircraft), land(착륙하다), a **landing** gear(착륙기어)

✷ get는 go/come의 의미를 동시에 갖는다. get on(타다), get off(=disembark), take on(=undertake, 맡다), take off(이륙하다; 벗다), call on(=ask; request), call off(=cancel), translate(통역하다)

한편, 동일한 단어에 부사 또는 전치사를 붙여 새로운 의미를 만들기도 한다. get에 on/off가 붙으면, (타다) **get on** the bus, (내리다) **get off** your bike가 된다. take의 경우는 (맡다) **take on** a project, (이륙하다) **take off** an airplane 또는 (벗다) **take off** your shoes가 된다. 내친 김에 call on/off에 대해서도 알아보자. call하여 on하면 ask(요청하다), off하면 cancel(취소하다)이 된다.

They **call on** me to translate it.

★ We had our trip to Spain **called off**.

✷ early(이른; 일찍), late(늦은; 늦게), lately(=recently, 최근), arrive → arrival, depart → departure, delay(=put off: postpone, 연기하다), delayed(=postponed), because of(=due to; owing to), baggage claim (수하물 찾는 곳), several bags; several pieces of baggage, claim(=pick up), to claim your bag

arrive는 come에, **depart**는 go/leave에 해당 된다. '도착'은 **arrival**, '출발'은 **departure**이다. baggage(수하물)는 '가방'(bags)을 의미.

★ How early should I **arrive** at the airport?

★ My flight **departs** an hour late.

★ Check your **arrival** and **departure** times.

★ Flights are **delayed** because of fog.

★ Pick it up at the **baggage** claim.

※ 빈칸에 적절한 단어를 써넣으시오.

01 He can take off and **l**______ an airplane.

02 Check your arrival and **d**______ times.

03 Flights are **d**______ or canceled because of fog.

04 How **e**______ should I arrive at the airport before my flight?

05 We had our trip to Spain **c**______ off because of the swine flu.

06 All the passengers of AF flight 447 to Paris, please **b**______ the flight.

07 My flight to India **d**______ an hour late. We'll do some souvenir shopping.

08 Pick it up at the **b**______ claim after disembarking from an airline flight.

09 I **f**______ from Incheon to Tokyo. What is the airport that is closer to the main Tokyo area?

10 Did you **b**______ a flight and hotel? If not, you can reserve a hotel when buying your airline tickets on KLM.com.

1. 그는 비행기를 이륙하고 착륙할 수 있다.
2. 도착과 출발 시간을 체크해요.
3. 항공편이 안개 때문에 지연되거나 취소됩니다.
4. 얼마나 일찍 공항에 도착해야 하나요.
5. 우리는 우리의 스페인 여행을 취소시켰다.
6. 비행기에 탑승하십시오.
7. 나의 인도 행 비행기는 1시간 늦게 출발한다.
8. 수하물 찾는 곳에서 그것을 찾으세요.
9. 나는 인천에서 도쿄로 비행기 타고 갑니다.
10. 항공편과 호텔을 예약하셨나요.

Answer

01. land
02. departure
03. delayed
04. early
05. called
06. board
07. departs
08. baggage
09. fly
10. book

※ 적절한 동사를 골라 써넣으시오.

board, book, fly, land

01 In a week he will __________ a ship bound for New York.

02 Many travelers plan to __________ a hotel room on their mobile device.

03 Is it cheaper to __________ to Paris from London or should I take the Eurostar?

04 Medical emergency forces a 70-passenger jet to __________ at a small airport.

※ 적절한 동사를 골라 써넣으시오.

arrived, cancelled, delayed, took

05 Their flight is __________ by two hours or more.

06 Forty departing flights were __________ due to heavy fog.

07 Only 80 percent of Auckland's trains __________ on time last month.

08 The plane __________ off from the Hillsboro Airport a minute ago.

1. in a week(일주일 후에), board (= get on) ≠ disembark, bound for(~행의)
2. 예약하다(book; reserve), mobile device(이동통신장치)
3. cheap/inexpensive / reasonable/expensive take a train/flight
4. land ≠take off, medical emergency(의료응급사태), passenger ≠ freight; cargo
5. 지연하다(delay; postpone; put off), 지연된(delayed; postponed)
6. arrive ≠ depart, 취소하다(cancel; call off), 취소되다(be cancelled), due to (= owing to; because of)
7. on time (= punctual; punctually)
8. land ≠ take off, take/took/taken

Answer

01. board
02. book
03. fly
04. land
05. delayed
06. cancelled
07. arrived
08. took

※ 적절한 명사를 골라 써넣으시오.

baggage, boarding, departure, delay

01 We have no time left for ________ or hesitation.

02 My bags never showed up. I couldn't find them at the ________ claim area.

03 We have a new system for flight arrival and ________ displays at the airport.

04 He flew from New York to Los Angeles with a stolen ________ pass and ID card.

※ 토픽에 해당하는 단어에 O표 하시오.

05 check-in/security/gate/airport/runway

06 Cairo/London/Canberra/Athens/Capital

07 Australia/Continent/Europe/Africa/Asia

08 Singapore/Country/Fiji/Malaysia/Finland

09 Holiday/Easter/Labor Day/Thanksgiving

10 car/transportation/bus/train/flight/cruise

1. hesitate (망설이다) → hesitation
2. show up(= appear), a bag (= a piece of baggage)
3. flight/airplane/plane, arrival ≠ departure
4. fly/flew/flown, ID(= identification, 신분증) steal/stole/stolen
5. security(방범; 보안), customs(세관)
6. capital(수도), captain(선장)
7. continent(대륙)
8. country(국가; 농촌)
9. Easter(부활절)
10. cruise(유람선), transportation(교통 수단)

Answer

01. delay
02. baggage
03. departure
04. boarding
05. airport
06. Capital
07. Continent
08. Country
09. Holiday
10. transportation

※ 괄호에 적절한 단어를 고르시오.

1. in the air
   ≠ on the ground
2. security(보안), 요구하다(claim)
3. 출발하다(set out on a journey; depart)
4. call off(=cancel), cancel → cancellation
5. am arriving(도착할 것이다), late(늦은; 늦게), lately(=recently), budget transport(저렴한 교통),
6. international
   ≠ domestic (국내의)
7. go on a trip(=take a trip), head for (~로 향하다), motorcycle → the Harley

01 Is the airplane on the (grind, ground) or in the air?

02 Please go through security and (claim, find) bags in Terminal C.

03 Three flights are scheduled to (depart, start) to Cancun from Pearson Airport.

04 If you plan to call off your wedding, you have to write a (cancel, cancellation) letter.

05 I am arriving (late, lately) at Haneda airport and have no idea on which budget transport to take.

06 Tokyo has two large airports : Narita for international flights, and Haneda for mostly (dome, domestic) flights.

07 (Go, Take) a road trip on a motorcycle. Pack your tent, sleeping bags, and the rest of your stuff on the Harley, and head for the open road.

Answer

01. ground
02. claim
03. depart
04. cancellation
05. late
06. domestic
07. Take

※ 괄호에 적절한 단어를 고르시오.

01 "Excuse me, excuse me, sorry, do you speak English? My car is broken down. I wonder if you could tell me where to find a garage." "I don't know what you are (saying, speaking)."

02 I often take flights to China. Year after year, I learn much knowledge about flights. A plane usually takes off and lands on time, but some reasons can cause a flight's (delay, delaying) or cancellation.

03 Why would airlines give away free tickets? More importantly how does it work?! First, you must understand that all major airlines overbook their flights. For example, if an American Airlines plane carries 100 people, they will sell 110 tickets, assuming that about 10% of them won't (get, show) up. A lot of people actually miss their flights because they arrived at the airport late, were too ill to travel, or simply changed their mind at the last minute.

1. speak English,
say something/yes,
tell a lie/the truth,
garage(차고; 자동차수리소)
2. often(= frequently),
take flights(= fly),
take off ≠ land,
cancel/cancellation,
delay/delay
3. airlines(항공사), give away
(나눠주다), work(작동되다),
overbook(초과 예약하다),
assume(가정하다),
about(= roughly),
show up(= appear),
late(늦게), lately(최근에),
ill(= sick),
change mind
(마음을 바꾸다)

Answer
01. saying
02. delay
03. show

② Countries and languages

※ <u>bi</u>lingual(= speaking <u>two</u> languages), mother tongue(모국어, first language; native language), <u>speak</u> the language, the language <u>is spoken</u> adore(= love very much), perform (공연하다)

당신은 English, Chinese, Japanese, Korean 중 2개 국어를 쓰고 있나요? 모국어는?

★ Are you **bilingual**?

What is your mother **tongue**?

★ Zhang Ziyi is a **Chinese** actress.

★ Ronak teaches **Arabic** language.

★ He gives me a **French** kiss.

★ Do you speak **German**?

★ I adore **Italian** food.

★ She works at a **Japanese** company.

★ **Korean** is spoken in Korea.

★ He is a **Russian** nuclear scientist.

★ See the **Spanish** dancer perform.

Britain; England; UK, USA; America, (.uk) ← United Kingdom, (.de) ← Deutschland, (.es) ← España

country	ccTLD	language
Brazil	.br	**Portuguese**
Britain	**.uk**	English
China	.cn	Chinese
Egypt	.eg	Arabic
France	.fr	French
Germany	**.de**	German
India	.in	English
Italy	.it	Italian
Japan	.jp	Japanese
Korea	.kr	Korean
New Zealand	.nz	English
Russia	.ru	Russian
Spain	**.es**	**Spanish**
USA	.us	English

※ ccTLD : country code top-level domain

※ 빈칸에 적절한 단어를 써 넣으시오.

01 **K**_________ is spoken in Korea.

02 He gives me a **F**_________ kiss.

03 Ronak teaches **A**_________ language at a muslim school.

04 I adore **I**_________ food. How do you make spaghetti meatballs?

05 Are you **b**_________? Can you speak more than two languages?

06 Zhang Ziyi is a **C**_________ actress. She is among the 4 major actresses in China.

07 See the **S**_________ dancer perform. The flamenco dancer was born in Madrid.

08 "Do you speak **G**_________?" I asked a friend of mine who traveled to Germany.

09 She works at a **J**_________ company, which pushes its people to work overtime instead of hiring additional staff.

10 Ivan is a **R**_________ nuclear scientist. The Soviet scientist denies being the brains behind Iran's nuclear program.

1. 한국어는 한국에서 말해집니다.
2. 그는 나에게 프렌치 키스를 한다.
3. 로낙은 아라비아어를 가르친다.
4. 나는 이탈리아 음식을 매우 좋아해요.
5. 당신은 2개 국어를 쓰나요.
6. 장쯔이는 중국의 여배우이다. Her first major role was in The Road Home (1999).
7. 그 스페인 댄서가 공연하는 것을 봐.
8. 당신은 독일어를 하세요.
9. 그녀는 일본 회사에서 일한다.
10. 아이반은 러시아의 핵 과학자입니다.

Answer

01. Korean
02. French
03. Arabic
04. Italian
05. bilingual
06. Chinese
07. Spanish
08. German
09. Japanese
10. Russian

※ 적절한 국명을 써넣으시오.

1. kiwi는 과일의 종류/새의 이름/New Zealand 사람을 지칭
2. in (도시 또는 국가)
3. hold a meeting /game, hold/held/held
4. the majority of(대다수의), delta(삼각주)
5. well-known(=famous; renowned), the 최상급 in 장소
6. English, Danish
7. Chinese, Japanese, Portuguese... because Brazil was a Portuguese colony
8. speak/spoke /spoken
9. mother tongue (=first language)
10. East → Eastern, dialect (방언)

01 **N**________ is famous for kiwi.

02 They eat a lot of spaghetti in **I**________.

03 The 2014 FIFA World Cup finals will be held in **B**________.

04 The majority of people in **E**________ live in the Nile valley and delta.

05 Vodka is one of the most well-known alcoholic drinks in **R**________.

※ 적절한 언어의 명칭을 써넣으시오.

06 People in Spain speak **S**________.

07 People speak **P**________ in Brazil.

08 **G**________ is spoken in Germany.

09 English and **F**________ are the mother tongues of Canadians.

10 All Middle Eastern countries speak **A**________ but different dialects.

Answer

01. New Zealand
02. Italy
03. Brazil
04. Egypt
05. Russia
06. Spanish
07. Portuguese
08. German
09. French
10. Arabic

※ 괄호에 적절한 것을 고르시오.

01 Do you speak (Italy/Italia/Italian)?

02 Beijing is the (cap/capital/top) of China.

03 I live in Paris. And (what/when/where) do you live?

04 He has (two, dual) nationality, coming from two countries.

05 I speak Korean and English, but no other (language/landing/voyage).

06 (Cairo, Lagos) is the largest city in the Arab world and Africa.

07 She travels (abroad/by road/foreign), to America and Europe, quite often.

08 South Korea hosted the G-20 Summit in (Sole, Seoul) in November, 2010.

09 (Tokyo, Yokohama) is the seat of the Government of Japan and home of the Emperor.

1. speak → language
2. capital(수도; 자본)
3. in Paris → 장소
4. nationality(국적), dual(= double), uni-/bi-/tri-/quadri-
5. I am bilingual. English/ Korean → language, voyage(항해)
6. Egypt의 수도. the 최상급 in 장소
7. abroad(해외로), often (= frequently)
8. host(주최하다), host ≠ guest, in(달; 연도), on(날짜)
9. seat (자리; 장소), emperor (황제)

01. Italian
02. capital
03. where
04. dual
05. language
06. Cairo
07. abroad
08. Seoul
09. Tokyo

※ 관계없는 하나의 단어에 X표 하시오.

01 taxi/train/take off/fly/land

02 early/late/on time/delayed/fly

03 plane/aircraft/plain/airplane/flight

04 gate/track/platform/runway/taxi stop

05 pilot/tower/stewardess/attendant/captain

※ 괄호에 적절한 단어를 고르시오.

06 For (domestic, international) travel, a passport is needed.

07 Can I make changes or (call, cancel) my reservation online?

08 We line up at the (gate, platform) before boarding a plane.

09 Trains have dining cars where (passengers, passers-by) can eat.

10 Round-trip airline tickets are sometimes less expensive than (single, one-way) tickets.

1. taxi (활주로로 서서히 이동하다)
2. on time (=punctual), early ≠ late
3. plain (평야; 못생긴)
4. 타는 곳이 아닌 것은? runway (활주로)
5. 항공기에 근무하는 사람이 아닌 것은? flight attendants (항공승무원)
6. dome(지붕), domestic (국내의)
7. cancel(= call off)
8. line up(줄서다), board(= get on), plane(= airplane; flight), gate(탑승구)
9. dining car (식당차), passer-by (지나가는 사람)
10. one-way (편도), round-trip (왕복)

Answer

01. train
02. fly
03. plain
04. runway
05. tower
06. international
07. cancel
08. gate
09. passengers
10. one-way

※ 괄호에 적절한 단어를 고르시오.

01 "What time should I arrive at the airport if my flight (parts, departs) at 7 a.m.?"

02 "Do I need to (pig, pick) up my luggage, go through customs and recheck it for my connecting flight?"

03 "Talk to the people at the airport, let them know you (lost, missed) your flight and ask for an alternative. They may put you on the next available flight."

04 I am traveling w/a Eurail pass and want to (serve, reserve) seats for an overnight train from Dresden, Germany to Zakopane, Poland with a train change in Wroclaw.

05 Today, I was on a small plane. A flight (attendee, attendant) told us that there was too much weight in the front of the plane and they needed three people to move to the back of the plane. I volunteered and walked to the back. She said, "Okay, we're going to need one more person."

1. at(건물 등 좁은 장소), at(시각)
2. luggage(= baggage), customs(세관), connecting flight(연결항공편)
3. alternative(대안; 다른 방법), available(이용가능한)
4. w/ (= with), reserve(= book), train change(환승)
5. 항공승무원(flight attendant), the front ≠ the back, volunteer(자원하다)

Answer

01. departs
02. pick
03. missed
04. reserve
05. attendant

※ 빈칸에 적절한 단어를 써넣으시오.

1. native language(= mother tongue), bi-(= two), multi(= many), language →lingual
2. (토픽) flight delay, lightning (번개), a flash of lightning, thunder (천둥), a crash of thunder, rattle (덜컹거림), cancel(= call off), prepare for(을 대비하다), lengthy(= long), in(도시/국가)
3. (토픽) language, speak (language)
4. (토픽) airport, once(한때; 한차례; 일단 ~하면), security(보안), departure board (출발전광판), ahead of schedule, on schedule, behind schedule, concourse(탑승구가 있는 큰 hall), navigate one's way(= go)

01 Jane is **b**_________. She grows up speaking her parents' native language of **Korean** in her childhood home while speaking **English** at school.

02 You see lightning and hear the thunder. If you can hear the rattle through the airport windows, you know the storm is too close for takeoff. Your flight may **not be canceled**, but you should prepare for a lengthy **d**_________.

03 There are many types of language around the world. In the United States we speak **English**, in Mexico they speak **S**_________ and in France they speak **French**. Believe it or not, there are well over 6,500 languages all around the world!

04 Go stand in line at the ticket counter to get your **b**_________ **pass**. Once you're through security, you' ll want to stop and check the departure board to make sure your flight is on schedule. Then, go find a map of the concourse so you can navigate your way to the gate.

Answer

01. bilingual
02. delay
03. Spanish
04. boarding

exercise 1

※ 적절한 동의어를 써넣으시오.

01 to take a flight = f________

02 to book a room = r________

03 to get on the train = b________

04 I pick up my bags. = c________

05 to call off wedding = c________

06 a piece of baggage = b________

07 flights are delayed = p________

08 a dancer from Spain = S________

09 They never show up. = a________

10 have lately bought it = r________

11 to depart from Tokyo = l________

12 speaking two languages = b________

1. go by air
2. booking (= reservation)
3. ≠ get off
4. (공항에서 짐)찾다
5. 취소하다
6. baggage(= bags), equipment(= tools)
7. put off(= postpone)
8. England/English, Denmark/Danish
9. 나타나다
10. buy/bought/bought, 최근에(lately; recently)
11. 떠나다
12. bi-(two), multi-(many)
13. famous(= well-known; renowned)
14. 수도

※ 괄호에 적절한 것을 고르시오.

13 (China, Russia) is famous for vodka.

14 Hanoi is the (capital, top) of Vietnam.

15. 공식어
16. captain (기장), land ≠ take off
17. get on ≠ get off
18. 늦은/늦게 (late)
19. board(= get on), proceed (= go forward)
20. reserve

15 English and French are the official (peoples, languages) in Canada.

16 This is your captain. We're going to (land, arriving) at the airport soon.

17 I was waiting at the bus stop for my children to (take, get) off the bus.

18 Several people arrived too (late, lately) to be admitted to the performance.

19 Passengers (getting, boarding) KE321 for Paris should proceed to Gate 9.

20 Many travelers (book, note) flights and hotels in a single package to save money.

My grade : ________/20

Test 1

ID :　　　　　　Name :

※ 주어진 단어를 사용하여 영어로 옮기시오.

01 항공편과 호텔을 예약하셨나요? (book)

____

02 항공편이 안개 때문에 지연되고 있습니다. (delay)

____

03 그는 비행기를 착륙시키는 법을 안다. (land)

____

04 도착과 출발 시간을 체크하세요. (arrival, departure)

____

05 수하물 찾는 곳에서 그것을 찾으세요. (pick up)

____

06 당신은 2개 국어를 쓰나요? (bilingual)

____

07 로낙은 아라비아어를 가르친다. (Ronak)

____

08 그는 나에게 프렌치 키스를 한다. (give a kiss)

____

09 당신은 독일어를 하세요? (speak)

____

10 그 스페인 댄서가 공연하는 것을 봐. (perform)

____

My grade : ________/10

Unit

02

Do a good job

Unit.

02 Do a good job

1 What are you doing?

job, work, apply, fire 등은 친숙한 단어이다. 쉽다고 여기겠지만, 주의할 점이 없지 않다. 먼저, job과 work 는 직무, 직업, 직장 등의 뜻으로 쓰이지만, work는 셀 수 없는 (some work), job은 셀 수 있는 명사(some jobs)다.

★ I have some **work** to do now.

★ You do **a good job**.

※ do/finish/start **work**, do/find/quit/lose **a job**, do **work**; do **a** good **job**, change **jobs**
You do a good job.
(=You work well.)

직업을 물을 때 다양한 표현이 있다.

★ What is your **occupation**?

What do you do for a living?

What are you doing?

※ occupy(점유하다) → occupancy(점유), occupation(직업), What is your occupation?은 매우 딱딱한 표현이다.

다음은 비자 인터뷰의 대화이다.
영사 : "What are you doing?"
틀린 대답 : "I'm being interviewed."
바른 대답 : I'm a mechanic/an office worker.

※ What are you doing?은 '무엇을 하고 있는 중입니까'의 뜻도 있어 간혹 오해를 낳는다.

※ what job (무슨 직무), Do you work shifts? (교대근무하세요), day/evening/night shift, full time ≠ part time

직무/근무형태를 물을 때에는

What job do you do?

★ Do you work **shifts**?

Do you work full time or part time?

How many hours a week do you work?

※ apply → application(지원서), applicant(= candidate), was offered(제안 받았다), accept ≠ refuse, am employed(고용 되다), employment(고용), recommendation(추천), is promoted(승진되다), promotion(승진), make a living(생계를 유지하다), live a happy life (행복한 삶을 살다)

다음으로 지원하다(apply for) 이외에 '채용/추천/승진하다'도 알아두자.

★ How many jobs did you **apply for**?

I **was offered** a better job after accepting one.

★ I am **employed**!

★ Please **recommend** me a gardener.

★ He is **promoted** to General Manager.

It is hard to **make a living** as a freelance writer.

※ blame(= scold; criticize; condemn), fire(= lay off; dismiss), close down(폐쇄하다), lay(= put), lay/laid/laid, lie (= be put), lie/lay/lain, employer(고용주), employee(종업원)

마지막으로, 일이 잘못되면 책망/해고가 있을 수도 있다. fire는 '해고하다' 이외에 '총쏘다/불지르다' 등 끔찍한 느낌을 주므로 대신에 lay off를 많이 쓴다. 어떤 사람을 직장에서 떼어내어(off) 멀리 둔다(lay)는 뜻이다.

★ The boss **blames** me for all his mistakes.

Can they **fire** me for being Korean?

★ We'll close down or **lay off** the workers.

All employees will be **dismissed** by April.

※ 빈칸에 적절한 단어를 써 넣으시오.

01 I am **e**__________! I have a job!

02 We'll close down or **l**__________ off the workers.

03 I have some **w**__________ to do before March arrives.

04 The boss **b**__________ me for all his mistakes. I am sick of it.

05 He is **p**__________ to General Manager. Let's congratulate him.

06 How many jobs did you **a**__________ for before you finally got an offer?

07 Please **r**__________ me a gardener who mows the lawn through the year.

08 Do you work **s**__________? Do you prefer to work nights to get some extra pay?

09 What is your **o**__________? Have you ever wondered what career matches your personality?

10 I am motivated to do a good **j**__________ because it gives me a good feeling and a sense of pride.

1. 나 채용됐어요!
2. 우리는 폐쇄하거나 노동자들을 해고시킬 것입니다.
3. 나는 지금 할 일이 좀 있어.
4. 사장은 자신의 모든 실수에 날 나무라요.
5. 그는 총지배인으로 승진된다.
6. 얼마나 많은 직장을 지원했어요.
7. 나에게 정원사를 추천해요.
8. 당신은 교대 근무하시나요.
9. 직업이 무엇이죠.
10. 동기부여 받아 일을 잘 하고 있어요.

Answer

01. employed
02. lay
03. work
04. blames
05. promoted
06. apply
07. recommend
08. shifts
09. occupation
10. job

※ 적절한 동사를 골라 써넣으시오.

blamed, do, employ, laid

1. often(=frequently), make a mistake/judgement/choice, 비난하다(blame; criticize; condemn)
2. lay/laid/laid, lay off(=fire; dismiss)
3. 고용하다(=hire), more than (=over), full time ≠ part time
4. always(=all the time), garage(차고; 자동차수리소), do a good job(=do a job well; work well)
5. lose ≠ find, lost and found (분실물 찾는 곳), 해고하다 (=fire; dismiss; lay off)
6. research online(=surf the internet)
7. ≠demoted, General Manager(총지배인)
8. change jobs(직장을 바꾸다), 입사하다 (join) ≠ resign; quit

01 My boss often __________ me for a mistake he made.

02 Three thousand workers are __________ off at the factory.

03 The project will __________ more than 250 full-time workers.

04 I always take my car to York garage. They __________ a good job.

※ 적절한 것을 골라 써넣으시오.

apply, fired, joining, promoted

05 I was __________. I was late so often and lost my job.

06 Pizzo and Hamm researched online to __________ for jobs.

07 She is __________. They make her General Manager from next month!

08 "I hear you're changing jobs." "Yes, I'm __________ an airline company."

Answer
01. blamed
02. laid
03. employ
04. do
05. fired
06. apply
07. promoted
08. joining

※ 괄호에 적절한 것을 고르시오.

01 Why do you apply (for, to) this position?

02 That's my final offer. Take it or (live, leave) it.

03 "What is your (hobby, occupation)?" "I'm a mechanic."

04 "What do you (do, work)?" "I teach at a primary school."

05 Do you really need a four-year degree for a good (job, work)?

06 The employees should work night (jobs, shifts) on the weekends.

07 A (part, full) time employee works between 7 and 10 hours a day.

08 Can you (commend, recommend) an applicant for a company of 90 employees?

09 I attend a garden party to celebrate his (promote, promotion) to branch manager.

1. 지원하다
2. take ≠ leave
3. occupant(점유자), occupation(직업), calling(천직)
4. primary(= elementary)
5. many jobs, much work
6. weekends ≠ weekdays
7. employee ≠ employer
8. commend(= praise), recommend(추천하다), applicant(= candidate), application(지원; 지원서)
9. attend(= go to) → attendance, celebrate(경축하다) → celebration promote (승진하다) → promotion

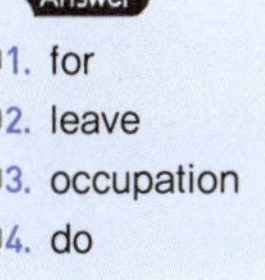

Answer

01. for
02. leave
03. occupation
04. do
05. job
06. shifts
07. full
08. recommend
09. promotion

※ 괄호에 적절한 단어를 고르시오.

01 He got a job at the record store in the shopping (mall, malt).

02 The art gallery is going to have an (open, opening) this evening.

03 This is our new (employee, employer). Please show him how to send a fax.

04 Today I go to the pharmacy, the hair salon and the (grocer, grocery) store.

05 The (butcher's shop, barbershop) put the beauty parlor out of business because it offered less expensive haircuts.

06 New Yorkers pretend to be the (idlest, busiest) people in the world. It seems like everyone is running to get somewhere and they're always running late.

07 We're starting to require a credit card to (do, make) an appointment, the same as if you're making hotel reservations. If you break the appointment without 24 hour notice, you will be charged an hourly rate based on the length of the anticipated appointment.

1. 상점가(= shopping mall; shopping center; shopping district; shopping street)
2. feel/feeling, open/opening ski/skiing
3. employee(종업원), employer(고용주)
4. pharmacy (약국), hair salon(= beauty parlor), grocer(식료품 장수), grocery(식료품)
5. butcher(푸줏간 주인), put out of business(망하게 하다)
6. pretend(~인 체하다), running → busy
7. make/break an appointment, reservation(= booking), charge(부과하다; 돌진하다), anticipate(기대하다)

Answer
01. mall
02. opening
03. employee
04. grocery
05. barbershop
06. busiest
07. make

※ 관계없는 하나의 단어에 X표 하시오.

01 gardener, grocer, jeweler, saucer

02 mechanic, magic, musician, physician

03 janitor, tailor, operator, beauty parlor

04 client, photocopier, typewriter, stapler

05 pants, dresses, bracelets, jeans, shorts

※ 반대 또는 대조되는 단어를 써넣으시오.

06 Are cell phones a **n**__________ or a **convenience**?

07 Put the **letter** in a large **e**__________ and stamp it.

08 I certify that this is a true **c**__________ of the **original** document.

09 A drop in the won-dollar exchange rate has sharply lowered **i**__________ and **export** costs.

10 This is one of the fast, reliable and convenient ways to **send** and **r**__________ money around the world.

1. cup and saucer
2. magic/magician
   music/musician
3. janitor(= custodian),
   beauty parlor(미장원)
4. client(고객),
   photocopier(복사기)
5. shorts(짧은 바지),
   bracelets(팔찌)
6. a convenience (편의용품)
7. staple and stapler,
   letter and envelope,
   stamp(우표붙이다)
8. certify(증명하다; 보증하다),
   original document(원본)
9. exchange rate (환율),
   lower ≠ raise, include and exclude, import and export, internal and external
10. convenient(편리한),
    send and receive,
    give and take

01. aucer
02. magic
03. beauty parlor
04. client
05. bracelets
06. necessity
07. envelope
08. copy
09. import
10. receive

② Occupations

※ a mechanic(자동차 수리공), fix(= repair; mend), mechanical(기계적), a critic(비평가), critical of(~에 비판적) Why are we so **critical of** others?

개개의 단어와 관련되는 말을 알아 두면, 독해는 물론 회화/작문에도 도움 된다. engine, bumper, jack, jump cable, test, tune, fix, cars, trucks 등의 단어가 나오면, 그 글은 an auto mechanic에 대한 것이다.

★ I pay a **mechanic** to fix my car.

My car has a **mechanical** problem.

※ cook(요리사)/cooker(조리기구), take advantage of(= use), surgeon(외과 의사) / surgery(수술), cheap cosmetic surgery (싸구려 미용성형)

사람과 사물을 구별하자.

The **cook** takes advantage of a slow **cooker**.

★ The **surgeon** practiced cheap cosmetic **surgery**.

※ take it or leave it, stay or go, succeed or fail, parents and children, nail and hammer, mop and bucket, cup and saucer, room and board, all or nothing, on and off, slowly but surely, sooner or later, blue and white collar workers

또한 단어엔 짝이 되는 말이 있다. 예를 들어,

★ Why do we **give** or **take** gifts?

★ **Groom** kisses **bride** after the vow.

★ The **host** greets **guests** at the door.

★ The **doctor** treats cancer **patients**.

★ The **lawyer** must know his **client**.

★ **Labor** and **management** work together.

★ Identify your **strengths** and **weaknesses**.

★ We are hiring for **domestic** and **international** call center executives.

※ 빈칸에 적절한 단어를 써 넣으시오.

01 I pay a **m**__________ to fix my car.

02 The doctor treats cancer **p**__________.

03 The host greets **g**__________ at the door.

04 Why do we give or **t**__________ gifts?

05 The surgeon practiced cheap cosmetic **s**__________ for two years.

06 Identify your **s**__________ and weaknesses for a job interview.

07 Do labor and **m**__________ work together to solve problems?

08 We're hiring for **d**__________ and international call center executives for India, US, UK and Australian process.

09 The **l**__________ must know his client. What should a defense attorney do if they know that their client is guilty?

10 The bride and **g**__________ kiss after the vows because it is like sealing the vows and celebrating the union they've made.

1. 내가 나의 차를 수리한 수리공에게 지불한다.
2. 그 의사는 암환자를 치료한다.
3. 초청자는 도어에서 손님을 영접한다.
4. 왜 우리는 선물을 주거나 받지.
5. 그 외과의사는 2년간 싸구려 미용성형을 실시했다.
6. 자신의 장단점을 확인하라.
7. 노동조합과 경영진은 협동하는가?
   labor (=union)
8. 국내/국제 콜센터의 간부를 고용할 것이다.
   hire(= employ)
9. 변호사는 의뢰인을 알아야 한다.
10. 서약 후 신부와 신랑은 키스 한다.

Answer

01. mechanic
02. patients
03. guests
04. take
05. surgery
06. strengths
07. management
08. domestic
09. lawyer
10. groom

※ 적절한 직업명을 골라 써넣으시오.

barber, carpenter, secretary, surgeon

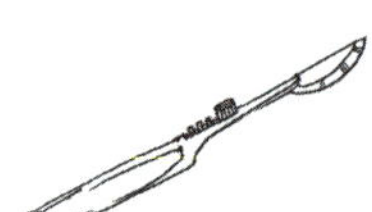

01 Mask, forceps, scissors and scalpel are used by a ___________.

02 Typewriter, filing cabinet and stapler are used by a ___________.

03 Saw, ruler, hammer and electric drill are used by a ___________.

04 Comb, scissors, clippers, mirror and hair brushes are used by a ___________.

※ 적절한 직업명을 골라 써넣으시오.

gardener, janitor, mechanic, police

05 My car wouldn't start this morning. I called a ___________.

06 A ___________ takes away garbage and cleans surfaces.

07 A ___________ waters and feeds plants, keeps bugs away from gardens.

08 ___________ patrol streets for traffic violators, hunt criminals, and answer distress calls.

1. forceps(핀셋, 집게), scalpel(외과용 메스)
2. staple을 삽입하여 stapler를 사용한다. secret (비밀)을 지키는 secretary(비서)
3. saw(톱), ruler(자)
4. clippers(이발기)
5. He uses jack, jump cable, etc.
6. 청소부(janitor; custodian), garbage(= trash; junk), clean up ≠ mess up
7. water(물주다), feed(먹이다), keep away(쫓다), bug(= pest, 해충)
8. patrol(순찰하다), violator(위반자), criminal(범인), distress call(조난신호)

Answer

01. surgeon
02. secretary
03. carpenter
04. barber
05. mechanic
06. janitor
07. gardener
08. Police

※ 적절한 것을 골라 써넣으시오.

employer, manager, strengths, union

01 You should identify your personal ________ and weaknesses.

02 Conflicts between ________ and employee escalated last year.

03 ________ is responsible for running a particular section of a business.

04 The need for a partnership between the ________ and the management will become more critical.

※ 괄호에 적절한 것을 고르시오.

05 How does he (do, make) a living as a musician?

06 Did the attorney meet obligations to his (client, customer)?

07 Do you expect your guests to say Hi! first or do you as the (host, owner) say Hi! first?

08 There are conflicts between labors and (manager, management) at the airline company.

1. identify(확인하다), weaknesses(단점) ≠ strengths
2. conflict(갈등), employee and employer, escalate(= go up)
3. responsible for(~에 책임 있는), run(= manage), a business(사업체)
4. critical (=very important)
5. live a life; make a living
6. attorney(= lawyer), meet(= satisfy), obligation(책무)
7. say hi(= greet), host and guest, bride and groom
8. conflict (충돌), labor(= union), management(경영진)

Answer

01. strengths
02. employer
03. Manager
04. union
05. make
06. client
07. host
08. management

※ 괄호에 적절한 것을 고르시오.

1. join (입사/입대하다), army/navy/marines/air force
2. leak(새다), send for(부르러 보내다), plumber(배관공)/plumbing(배관)
3. call in sick(아프다고 전화하다)
4. janitor(= custodian), plumber(배관공), attend to(돌보다)
5. gift (재능), vehicle (차량)
6. physician(내과의사), surgeon(외과의사), social worker(사회 복지사), family issue(가족문제)
7. doctor and patient, lawyer and client
8. pastor(목사), in blue(푸른 옷을 입은) bride and groom

01 "Jane joins the army." "My son is a (shoulder, soldier) too."

02 The pipe is leaking. We have to send for a (mechanic, plumber).

03 Service in the cafe was slow. One (cook, cooker) called in sick.

04 (Janitor, Plumber) attends to the maintenance or cleaning of a building.

05 He has the gift of fixing vehicles, going to open a (mechanic, mechanical) shop.

06 (Physicians, Social workers) help others with everyday problems, their relationships and family issues.

07 100 year-old Ohio doctor still treats (patience, patients). He goes to see them if they're sick and can't leave home.

08 "Dearly beloved, we are gathered here together in the presence of God …" the pastor of Prospect Park Methodist church speaks to the bride and (gloom, groom), both of whom are dressed in dark blue.

Answer

01. soldier
02. plumber
03. cook
04. Janitor
05. mechanic
06. Social workers
07. patients
08. groom

※ 관련 없는 하나의 단어에 X표 하시오.

01 doctor/teacher/manufacturer/nurse

02 caddie/gardener/lawyer/farmer/porter

03 butcher/mayor/governor/official/police

04 accountant/baker/banker/cashier/teller

05 barber/nurse/orderly/surgeon/technician

1. work with people
2. work outside
3. work in government 관련. butcher (푸줏간 주인)
4. working with money 관련. teller (수납계원)
5. hospital 관련. orderly(병원 심부름꾼)
6. early or late, earlier(=sooner)
7. distant(=far), now and then (=sometimes; not very often)
8. 육체노동자/사무원
9. 확실히
10. the rich(=rich people), give and take

※ 짝이 되는 단어를 써넣으시오.

06 He'll pay the bill **sooner** or **l**__________.

07 People came from **near** and **f**__________ to see the Pope.

08 Do all **blue** collar workers think **w**__________ collar workers don't work?

09 Nancy is finishing the paint job on her house, **slowly** but **s**__________.

10 **T**__________ from the rich and **give** to the less rich. That's Governor John Liu's plan.

Answer

01. manufacturer
02. lawyer
03. butcher
04. baker
05. barber
06. later
07. far
08. white
09. surely
10. Take

※ 괄호에 적절한 것을 고르시오.

1. divide → division, shift(교대근무), midnight (24시), noon (12시)
2. do something/nothing/little, welcome respite(환대받는 휴식), at first ≠ at last, you're about to(~하는 참이다), lay off(= dismiss; fire), colleague(= co-worker)
3. greet(인사하다), the first impression(첫인상), promptly(즉각), within the first three rings (벨이 세 번 울리기 전에), assist(= help, 도와주다), assistance(도움), appropriate(적절한), inappropriate(부적절한)

01 A day may be divided into three (parts, shifts), each of 8 hours, and each employee works just one of the followings : midnight to 08:00, 08:00 to 16:00, and 16:00 to midnight.

02 Suddenly finding yourself with little to do at the office may seem like a welcome respite at first, but it's also one of the signs you're about to be (lay, laid) off. If no work is coming in, why does your employer have to keep you and your colleagues around?

03 Your greeting may be the first impression a caller receives of your company. Answer the phone promptly, within the first three rings. Clearly state a greeting that includes the name of your company, your name and an offer of (assist, assistance). For example, an appropriate greeting would be, "Good morning, you have reached Apex Company. This is Melody speaking. How may I help you?"

Answer
01. shifts
02. laid
03. assistance

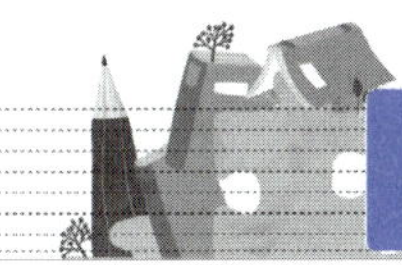

exercise 2

※반대/대조의 말을 써넣으시오.

01	to blame me	≠p________	1. 책망하다
02	to take a test	≠g________	2. give and take
03	He is employed.	≠u________	3. unemployment
04	your occupation	≠h________	4. occupation(직업)
05	to see a doctor	≠p________	5. bodily
06	to greet guests	≠h________	6. greet(환대하다)
07	I gave you all.	≠n________	7. 모든 것(=everything)
08	my only weakness	≠s________	8. weak ≠ strong
09	a blue collar worker	≠w________	9. manual worker
10	international markets	≠d________	10. 국제적≠국내의
11	in conflict with unions	≠m________	11. 노동조합
12	to resign from your job	≠k________	12. 사퇴하다
			13. 승진되다(get promoted)
			14. do work/a good job

※ 괄호에 적절한 것을 고르시오.

13 He got (promote, promoted) today.

14 I want to (do/make) that kind of work.

15. lay off(=fire), pregnancy (임신), lay/laid/laid
16. lawyer/ client, shopkeeper/ customer
17. critic(=reviewer)
18. hire(=employ)
19. apply → application(지원서)
20. commend(=praise), recommend(추천하다)

15 Are you (lay/laid) off because of your pregnancy?

16 We lawyers truly care about our (clients/customers).

17 He is the first film (critic, critical) to win a Pulitzer Prize.

18 How soon can we (fire/hire) a new employee to replace one that we laid off?

19 They accept an (apply/application) for summer and fall internship positions.

20 What restaurants will you (commend, recommend) for someone who likes wine?

My grade : ________/20

Test 2

ID :　　　　　　Name :

※ 주어진 단어를 사용하여 영어로 옮기시오.

01 나는 지금 할 일이 좀 있어. (some work)

___

02 당신은 일을 잘해. (do a job)

___

03 얼마나 많은 직장을 지원했어요? (apply for)

___

04 저에게 정원사를 추천해주세요. (a gardener)

___

05 사장은 자신의 모든 실수에 날 나무라요. (all his mistakes)

___

06 나는 내 차를 수리한 수리공에게 지불한다. (fix)

___

07 신랑은 서약 후 신부에게 키스한다. (after the vow)

___

08 초청자는 도어에서 손님을 영접한다. (greet)

____

09 변호사는 의뢰인을 반드시 알아야 한다. (the lawyer)

____

10 당신의 장점과 단점을 확인하라. (identify)

____

My grade : ________/10

Unit

03

Watch me grow

Unit.

03 Watch me grow

1 Trust me

신뢰는 인품(character)의 중요한 요소. 누구를 믿거나, 이야기를 의심하고 있다면,

★ I **believe in** you.

★ **Trust** me. You won't regret it.

★ The police **doubt** your story.

You **lie** to me.

✳ believe in(= count on; trust), won't(= will not), regret(후회하다), people/cattle/fish/ the police는 복수취급, doubt(= disbelieve), lie/lied/lied, lie ≠ tell the truth

'참다' 역시 중요한 미덕이다.

★ I have to grin and **bear** it.

She **stood** his rude behavior.

Why do you **put up with** his bad behavior?

✳ have to(= must), grin(씩 웃다), bear(= stand; tolerate), bear/bore/borne, stand/stood/stood, rude(= impolite), put up with(= tolerate), behave → behavior(행위)

우리는 첫 데이트, 시험, 취업면접 등의 경우 초조하거나(nervous) 우왕좌왕한다(panic).

★ You look so nervous. **Calm down**.

★ When I saw he wasn't breathing I **panicked**.

✳ calm(= make quiet; become quiet; cool off; relax) ≠ panic, breath (호흡) → breathe (호흡하다)

✷ grow/grew/grown,
grow up(자라다),
※ bring up(=raise, 키우다)

우리는 상대방에게 '성장을 지켜봐 주세요,' '철 좀 들어'라고 말하는 경우가 더러 있다.

★ **Watch** me grow.

★ Please **grow up**.

✷ find/found/found,
과거분사(trapped),
현재분사(talking),
I **felt** myself thrown into the air.
She **noticed** someone following her.

위의 watch는 지각동사(see, hear, find, feel, notice 등). 동사원형 이외에 과거분사, 현재 분사 등 다양한 목적격보어를 갖는다.

★ We found <u>him</u> **trapped** under the car.

★ Can you hear <u>me</u> **talking**?

〈상태 동사 + 형용사〉

상태동사에는 be동사유형과 become동사유형의 두 가지가 있다. 먼저, be동사유형에는 be(am, are, is), remain, stay, appear, look, smell, taste, feel, sound, seem 등이 있다. 예를 들면,

1. I **am** awake. I **remain** awake. I **stay** awake.
2. You **are** nice. You **look** nice. You **smell** nice.
3. The pie **is** sweet. It **appears** sweet. It **tastes** sweet.
4. This knife **is** heavy. It **feels** heavy. It **weighs** 10 kilograms.
5. His story **is** interesting. It **sounds** interesting. It **seems** interesting.

(continued on page 59)

※ 괄호에 적절한 것을 고르시오.

1. Mrs Oliver remained (silent, silently).
2. Can arthritis appear (sudden, suddenly)?
3. The food smelled (delicious, deliciously).
4. She behaved more (reasonable, reasonably).
5. The patient seems more (live, lively) today.
6. You should stay (quiet, quietly) during a meeting.
7. He appears (happy, happily) and confident this morning.

Answers

1. silent 2. suddenly 3. delicious 4. reasonably 5. lively 6. quiet 7. happy

※ 빈칸에 적절한 단어를 써 넣으시오.

01 I have to grin and **b**__________ it.

02 **W**__________ me grow as an artist.

03 **T**__________ me. You won't regret it.

04 You look so nervous. **C**__________ down.

05 Sarah, please **g**__________ up, shut up or go away.

06 The police **d**__________ your story about kidnapping.

07 I **b**__________ in you, I can trust in you forever. And I won't fear.

08 I just got this cell phone a couple days ago. Can you hear me **t**__________?

09 When I saw my son wasn't breathing

I **p**__________, I didn't know what to do.

10 We **f**__________ him trapped under the car. He was unconscious and his arm was caught over his chest.

1. 나는 웃어넘기며 참아야 해.
2. 제가 성장하는 것을 지켜 봐 주세요.
3. 나를 믿어줘. 후회하지 않을 거야.
4. 초조해보여. 진정해.
5. 철 좀 들어.
6. 경찰은 당신의 이야기를 의심하고 있다.
7. 나는 널 신뢰한다.
8. 당신은 내가 말하는 것을 들을 수 있나요.
9. 나는 공황상태에 빠졌어요.
10. 우리는 그가 자동차 아래 갇혀 있는 것을 발견했다.

Answer

01. bear
02. Watch
03. Trust
04. Calm
05. grow
06. doubt
07. believe
08. talking
09. panicked
10. found

※ 적절한 동사를 골라 써넣으시오.

calm, panicked, tolerate, trust

1. run/ran/run, calm down(≠panic)
2. (believe in; trust) ≠ mistrust, not any more (=no more)
3. had to (must의 과거형), bad⟨terrible ⟨awful, bear (= stand; tolerate)
4. nerve(신경) → nervous(초조한), relax(= cool off; calm)
5. 참다(bear; stand; put up with), noise(소음), not any longer(= no longer)
6. blame(= disapprove; condemn) ≠ praise, still (여전히; 잠잠한)
7. 후회하다(regret; feel sad), choose → choice (선택)
8. worth(=worthy of), 참다(bear; stand; put up with), bad smell(= odor)

01 I __________ and ran from the accident.

02 He often lies. I just don't __________ him any more.

03 They had to __________ awful working conditions for years.

04 You look so nervous. Please __________ down. Nothing bad is going to happen.

※ 적절한 동사를 골라 써넣으시오.

believe, put, regret, stand

05 I couldn't __________ up with the noise any longer.

06 Everybody blames her, but I will still __________ in her.

07 I will never __________ my choice to become a nurse.

08 Not worth crying over, but I can't __________ the bad smell of the floor mat in the car.

Answer

01. panicked
02. trust
03. tolerate
04. calm
05. put
06. believe
07. regret
08. stand

※ 괄호에 적절한 것을 고르시오.

01 I (heard, listened) her say that.

02 He noticed (I, me) ignored him.

03 I (rely, believe) upon you to do a good job.

04 After the fight both men need to (put, cool) off.

05 But I will trust him, believe him, never (doubt, dot) him.

06 Does he (grow, bring) up to be a famous but penniless composer?

07 I was spying on my neighbor and found (he, him) doing something illegal.

08 They (lay, lied) to cover up their mistakes and bad behavior yesterday.

09 The best way to (calm, come) down a frightened child is to pick her up and hold her.

1. 지각동사(see, hear, find, notice 등) … .+ 동사원형/현재분사
2. notice + that 절, ignore (무시하다)
3. depend on/count on /rely on, do a good job(= work well)
4. put off(=postpone; delay), cool off(= calm down; become quiet)
5. trust(= not doubt)
6. grow up(성숙하다), bring up(양육하다), composer(작곡가)
7. spy on(염탐하다), legal ≠ illegal
8. lie(놓여있다)/lay/lain, lie(거짓말하다)/lied/lied, make mistakes, cover up mistakes; hide mistakes, admit mistakes,
9. frightened (=scared; very afraid)

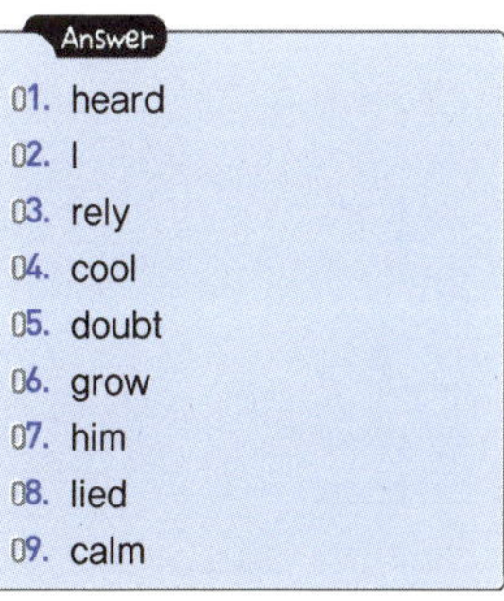
Answer

01. heard
02. I
03. rely
04. cool
05. doubt
06. grow
07. him
08. lied
09. calm

※ 빈칸에 짝이 되는 단어를 써넣으시오.

1. love or hate
2. fail or succeed
3. calm(=cool off)
4. trust or doubt
5. have on(=wear), 앞뒤를 거꾸로(back to front), 안팎을 뒤집어(inside out)
6. all or nothing, in return (보답으로)
7. hang/hung/hung, 위아래를 거꾸로(upside down)
8. 보내고 받고
9. traditional/modern, wedding(결혼식), ceremony(의례), 신부와 신랑
10. warning(경고), youngsters(청소년), tell a lie ≠ tell the truth

01 Do you **love** my short hair or **h**__________ it?

02 Do you need to **fail** before you **s**__________?

03 How do I **calm** myself during a **p**__________ attack?

04 I can't **trust** her. I **d**__________ everything she says.

05 Nancy, you have your sweater on **back** to **f**__________.

06 I gave you **all** my love and got **n**__________ in return.

07 The painting was hung **up**side **d**__________ for 47 days in the museum.

08 We **send** or **r**__________ text messages on our mobile phones every day.

09 In traditional Catholic weddings, as well as most European ceremonies, the **b**__________ and **groom** walk together.

10 The story of Pinocchio, whose nose grew when he told a **lie**, has served as a warning to youngsters to tell the **t**__________.

Answer

01. hate
02. succeed
03. panic
04. doubt
05. front
06. nothing
07. down
08. receive
09. bride
10. truth

※ 관계없는 하나의 단어에 X표 하시오.

01 stand/bear/endanger/tolerate/endure

02 happy/satisfied/content/depressed/glad

03 prior/freshman/sophomore/junior/senior

04 thankful/grateful/dissatisfied/appreciating

05 honest/trustworthy/truthful/sincere/lying

1. 참다
2. 만족하는
3. 1/2/3/4학년
4. 감사하는
5. 정직한; 성실한
6. happy/unhappy
7. honest/dishonest
8. 의심하다(suspect), 신뢰하다(trust; count on)
9. 너저분한(messy), 정돈된(orderly; organized)
10. present or absent, take (점검하다), attendance(출석)

※ 반대 또는 대조되는 단어를 써넣으시오.

06 Is the cab driver **friendly** or **u**________?

07 Are you a **satisfied** or **d**________ customer?

08 I used to **t**________ Chris but I'm now starting to **suspect** his actions.

09 Are you ok with a **messy** house, or are you rather **o**________ and clean?

10 Everyday the teacher takes attendance by marking which students are **present** and which are **a**________.

Answer
01. endanger
02. depressed
03. prior
04. dissatisfied
05. lying
06. unfriendly
07. dissatisfied
08. trust
09. orderly
10. absent

② A reliable person

✱ reliable(= dependable; trustworthy; trusted), grateful = thankful, punctual (= on time), patient ≠ impatient, talkative ≠ shy thoughtfu l≠thoughtless decisive ≠ indecisive selfish ≠ unselfish

형용사는 독특한 형태의 접미어를 갖는다.

reliable/reasonable, patient/brilliant, nervous/generous, decisive/talkative, foolish/selfish, grateful/thoughtful, emotional/punctual

★ He is a **reliable** leader.

★ My teacher was **patient** with me.

★ Mary talks a lot. She is **talkative**.

★ I am **grateful** for your help.

✱ satisfied with; surprised at; scared of, satisfied ≠ dissatisfied, move는 '움직이다' 외에도 '감동하다'의 뜻도 있다. This is a moving success story. I am moved by the story.

일부의 경우 동사의 … ing/ …ed형이 형용사로 쓰인다.

interesting/interested, satisfying/satisfied, surprising/surprised, scaring/scared, moving/moved,

★ It's a very **interesting** but stupid story.

★ You are **interested in** him.

He made a **surprising** discovery.

I was **surprised** at the news.

✱ live concert(생중계의 콘서트), he is alive(그는 살아 있다). she is lively(그녀는 생기 있다). wicked(= very bad), broad ≠ narrow, friendly ≠ unfriendly,

또한 명사에 …ed/ …ly/ …y를 붙여

wicked, broad-minded, friendly, orderly, lively, costly, funny, hungry, angry

★ I made a **wicked** attempt to steal it.

★ We have to be **broad-minded**.

★ I need some **friendly** advice.

★ My desk is always **messy**.

messy ≠ orderly
an orderly room
yearly (=annual),
costly (=expensive)

(continued from page 52)

〈상태 동사 + 형용사〉

상태동사 중 become동사의 유형에는 become, grow, get, go, prove, turn 등이 있다. 예를 들면,

1. I **become** strong. I **grow** strong. I **get** strong.
2. My black hair **became** grey. It **went** gray.
3. This information **became** useful. It **proved** useful.
4. The milk **became** sour. It **turned** sour.

※ 괄호에 적절한 것을 고르시오.

1. Why does hair turn (grey, greyly)?
2. He loved it so much. He went (mad, madly).
3. I feel dizzy when I get (hungry, hungrily).
4. He became (health, healthy) after the operation.
5. How (quick, quickly) does grape juice turn to wine?
6. Are you growing (impatient, impatiently) with someone?
7. He jumped up from his seat, and went (quick, quickly) to the station.

Answers

1. grey 2. mad 3. hungry 4. healthy 5. quickly 6. impatient 7. quickly

※ 빈칸에 적절한 단어를 써 넣으시오.

1. 나는 당신 도움에 감사해요.
2. 나는 그것을 훔치는 사악한 시도를 했다.
3. 그것은 흥미롭지만 우스꽝스런 이야기다.
4. 그녀는 수다쟁이다.
5. 내 책상은 항상 엉망입니다.
6. 나는 우정의 충고가 좀 필요해.
7. 당신이 그에 관심 있어.
8. 그는 믿고 의지할 수 있는 지도자다.
9. 나의 선생은 나에게 인내심이 있어요.
10. 우리는 너그러워야 한다.

01 I am **g**__________ to you for your **help**.

02 I made a **w**__________ attempt to **steal** it.

03 It is an **i**__________ **but** stupid story.

04 She is **t**__________. She really has a **big mouth**.

05 My desk is always **m**__________! I'm too lazy to **clean up**.

06 I would like to lose weight. I need some **f**_______ **advice**.

07 Let him know you are **i**__________ **in** him as soon as possible.

08 People **trust** and follow him because he is a **r**__________ and trustworthy leader.

09 My teacher is **p**__________ with me. I like him because he listens to what I say and takes me seriously.

10 We have to be **b**__________. We will have firm opinions, but will **be open** to hearing other people's opinions.

Answer
01. grateful
02. wicked
03. interesting
04. talkative
05. messy
06. friendly
07. interested
08. reliable
09. patient
10. broad-minded

※ 적절한 형용사를 골라 써넣으시오.

impatient, messy, punctual, reliable

01 My mom was __________ with me, yelling "Come here··· NOW."

02 We should not keep others waiting for us. We must be __________.

03 The boss counts on his assistant to do the work. She is very __________.

04 Bedrooms often become __________. Clothes, shoes, books and trash can pile up and become scattered about the room.

※ 적절한 형용사를 골라 써넣으시오.

big-headed, orderly, unreliable, wicked

05 Let me tell you how to handle __________ people you can't depend on.

06 His desk is always full, but he keeps it neat and __________.

07 She's so __________. She's always telling us how well she plays the guitar.

08 He finally made a __________ attempt to steal money from his mother.

1. ≠ patient(= tolerant), yell (고함치다), happy/satisfied/familiar/impatient with
2. early/late/punctual, punctual(= on time)
3. count on(= trust; rely on), assistant(= helper), do work(= do a job)
4. disorderly and dirty (= messy), pile up(쌓이다), scattered(흩어진)
5. handle(= deal with), depend on(= rely on), dependable(= reliable)
6. full ≠ empty, order(질서), orderly(정돈된; 심부름꾼)
7. 잘난체하는(conceited; bigheaded) ≠ modest
8. wicked(= bad; evil, 사악한)

Answer
01. impatient
02. punctual
03. reliable
04. sensitive
05. unreliable
06. orderly
07. big-headed
08. wicked

※ 적절한 형용사를 골라 써넣으시오.

boring, generous, grateful, honest

1. thankful for
2. tell a lie; tell the truth, honest ≠ dishonest, an honest man
3. 관대한(= generous; kind-hearted; broad-minded)
4. exciting ≠ boring
5. friendly(≠ hostile; unfriendly)
6. reliable(= dependable)
7. evil(= wicked; very bad)
8. past(과거), suspicious(= doubtful)
9. costly(= expensive)
10. thankful(= grateful)

01 I am so ________ for my husband's support.

02 Jacob is ________. He's telling the truth to others.

03 My husband is so ________. He is always buying me things.

04 My life is ________. How can I have a fun and exciting life?

※ 적절한 형용사를 써넣으시오.

05 비우호적 He is **u**________.

06 의지할 만한 a **d**________ car

07 사악한 a **w**________ habit

08 의심스런 his **d**________ past

09 비싼 her **c**________ coat

10 감사하는 I am **g**________ to you.

Answer

01. grateful
02. honest
03. generous
04. boring
05. unfriendly
06. dependable
07. wicked
08. doubtful
09. costly
10. grateful

※ 괄호에 적절한 것을 고르시오.

01 I talk a lot. I am (shy, talkative).

02 Don'tt be (mean, meaning) to me. I can't take it.

03 To be honest, I am (doubt, doubtful) of your success.

04 Today, the nation awaits (deciding, decisive) leadership.

05 Physicians are (satisfied, satisfying) with hospital chaplain services.

06 How can I let a guy know I am (interested, interesting) in him?

07 A good teacher must be (patient, impatient), with gentle but firm voice, can go down to the level of his pupils and willing to learn from them.

08 (Honest, Honesty) is important. That is the only way for you to gain trust from others. If you are always known for lying then nobody will ever trust you.

1. 수다스런 ≠ shy
2. 참다[take; stand; mean (=unkind), bear; tolerate].
3. be 아래에 형용사. careful/doubtful of
4. await(=wait for), decisive ≠indecisive
5. physician(의사; 내과의사), surgeon(외과의사), chaplain(전속목사)
6. involved/interested in
7. he is patient와 he is a patient의 차이점을 알죠?
8. difficult → difficulty, jealous → jealousy, honest → honesty, gain ≠ lose, known for(=famous for), trust(=believe in), lie → lying, die → dying, picnic → picnicking

Answer

01. talkative
02. mean
03. doubtful
04. decisive
05. satisfied
06. interested
07. patient
08. Honesty

※ 괄호에 적절한 단어를 고르시오.

1. rude (=impolite)
2. big-headed (잘난 체 하는), modest(겸손한), humble(겸손한; 초라한)
3. worried(= concerned) 인 것으로 보아 지루한?
4. honourable(명예로운)
5. 단호한(decisive), 우유부단한(indecisive), convey(= deliver)
6. seldom(거의 않다), punctual(= on time), work (직장), I've(= I have), constantly(= always), struggle(고투하다), punctuality(시간 정확성), make it(= succeed)
7. seek ≠ hide, receptionist (접수계원), behavior(= demeanor), excellent(= very good), candidate(= applicant), dependable(= reliable), 16-20 hours → part time job

01 I was an extremely (patient, impatient) and rude person.

02 He is a humble and (big-headed, modest) individual.

03 I'm actually worried that my life is becoming (boring, interesting).

04 I am an (honest, honourable) man and don't believe in lying to anyone.

05 Matty needed to be (decisive, indecisive), to convey strong leadership.

06 I'm seldom punctual for work. I've been working for 8 years now but I constantly struggled with punctuality. On most days, I would 'just make it' (in, on) time.

07 We're seeking a (full, part) time front office receptionist with a very friendly behavior and excellent customer service skills. Candidates should be highly dependable and (reliable, doubtful). Position will be 16-20 hours a week with evening hours and a full day on Friday.

Answer
01. impatient
02. modest
03. boring
04. honest
05. decisive
06. on
07. part, reliable

exercise 3

※ 동의어/반의어를 써넣으시오.

01 I believe in you. = t________

02 a dependable car = r________

03 a very bad world = w________

04 I'm grateful to you. = t________

05 He is kind-hearted. = g________

06 She is shy. ≠ t________

07 He panicked. ≠ c________

08 a messy desk ≠ o________

09 to tell the truth ≠ l________

10 friendly with me ≠ u________

11 to trust his story ≠ d________

12 My boss is big-headed. ≠ m________

1. 신뢰하다
2. 믿을 수 있는
3. evil
4. 감사하는(appreciative)
5. broad-minded
6. 말없는
7. 우왕좌왕하다
8. 정돈된(organized; orderly)
9. 거짓말하다?
10. ≠ 비우호적
11. 신뢰하다
12. 잘난체하는
13. find … alive/dead
14. bring up(= raise)

※ 괄호에 적절한 것을 고르시오.

13 I (found, discovered) him still alive.

14 What job will you have when you (bring, grow) up?

15. withstand(= resist), rude ≠ polite
16. swing(휘두르다)
17. 관심 있는
18. scream(비명지르다)
19. complain(불평하다) → complaint
20. admit(인정하다), deny(부정하다), chop down(베어 넘어뜨리다)

15 I can't (stand, withstand) him because of his rude behavior.

16 She continued to swing (wild, wildly) at the masked man.

17 Why are you (interested, interesting) in working for our company?

18 Neighbors (heard, listened) the child screaming and called the police.

19 They waited for hours without complaining. They're (patient, impatient).

20 I can't tell a (lie, tale) : I neither admit nor deny I chopped down the cherry tree.

My grade : ________ /20

Test 3

ID :　　　　　　Name :

※ 주어진 단어를 사용하여 영어로 옮기시오.

01 나는 널 신뢰하고 있어. (believe)

____

02 나를 믿어줘. 후회하지 않을 거야. (trust, regret)

____

03 너 참 초조해보여. 진정해. (calm down)

____

04 나는 공황상태였어. (panic)

____

05 당신은 내가 말하고 있는 것을 들을 수 있어요? (talking)

____

06 그는 믿을 수 있는 지도자다. (reliable)

____

07 나는 당신 도움에 감사해요. (grateful)

____

08 당신은 그에게 관심 있습니다. (interested in)

____

09 나는 약간의 우정의 충고가 필요해. (some advice)

____

10 나의 책상은 항상 너저분하다. (messy)

____

My grade : ________ /10

Unit

04

Look good

Unit.

04 Look good

① What does she look like?

우리는 외모(appearance)를 키, 몸무게, 나이 등으로 묘사하곤 한다. 키가 작은(short)/ 중간(medium)/큰(tall)

★ She is **medium height**.

★ He is a strong and **muscular** guy.

How **tall** is he?

※ high → height, muscle → muscular (= well-built), circle → circular(= round), He is 6 feet **tall**. He stands 6 feet.

날씬(slim)/뚱뚱(overweight)하면,

★ She was a smart **slim** and beautiful girl.

★ I am a little **overweight**.

Women **gain weight** after marriage.

★ Does he **weigh** over 100 kilograms?

※ thin(여윈)/lean(마른)/ **slim**(날씬)/plump(통통)/ **overweight**(뚱뚱)/ fat(비계의)/obese(비만의). gain weight(= put on weight), lose weight(= shed weight), Is he over 100 kg **in weight**.

잘/잘못 생겼으면

★ Is she **pretty** or **plain**?

You look **gorgeous** today.

★ Who does your baby **look** more **like**, mother or father?

※ ugly/plain/pretty/ beautiful/gorgeous ← gorge (계곡), plain (못생긴) ← plain (평야), look like(= resemble)

※ little(= small, 초등 하급반 연령), 젊은(young/ junior), youths(= adolescents), 중년의(= middle-aged), 늙은(old/**aged**/senior), the elderly(= the old; old people; senior citizen)

나이(age)가 어린(little)/젊은(young)/늙은(old)은 알겠는데, 청년? 중년? 노년?

★ Three out of ten **youths** drink too much.

★ A **middle-aged** man is seen wandering around.

★ Half **the elderly** take these drugs.

〈의문문의 유형〉

흔히 쓰이는 의문문에는 1) Yes/No Questions, 2) Alternative Questions, 3) Information Questions 등이 있다. 예를 들면,

1) "Are you married?" "**Yes**, I am."
2) "Which do you prefer, coffee **or** tea?" "I like coffee."
3) "**What** does she look like?" "She has black and wavy hair."

(continued to page 152)

※ 빈칸에 적절한 단어를 써넣으시오.

1. "_______ color is your bag?" "Red."
2. "Is your car blue?" "_______, it's red."
3. "_______ much time do you need?" "About two weeks."
4. "_______ can I get it?" "From the machine over there."
5. "How _______ do you visit your parents?" "Once a week."
6. "Who makes the decisions in your office?" "Mr. Park _______."
7. "Do I respond by email _______ send a letter?" "It doesn't matter."
8. "_______ does the store close so early?" "Because of the holiday."
9. "Should I call him _______ would you rather contact him?" "I'll call him."
10. "Isn't there a vending machine around here?" "_______, there is one at the other end of the hall."

Answers

1. What 2. No 3. How 4. Where 5. often 6. does 7. or 8. Why 9. or 10. Yes

※ 빈칸에 적절한 단어를 써넣으시오.

01 Is she pretty or **p**__________?

02 He **w**__________ about 100 kilograms.

03 Ella looks **l**__________ her mother very much.

04 "How tall is she?" "She is medium **h**__________."

05 Namitha was a beautiful actress when she was **s**__________ during her debut films.

06 I am a little **o**__________. What is the best way to actually lose weight?

07 He's a strong and **m**__________ guy. Are you attracted to the well-built man?

08 Half the **e**__________ take these drugs which are linked to mental decline.

09 Why do young people drink alcohol? Three out of 10 **y**__________ drink too much.

10 A **m**__________-aged man is seen wandering around. He's over 40 years old.

1. 그녀는 예쁜가요, 못생겼나요.
2. 그는 체중이 대략 100kg이다.
3. 엘라는 그녀의 어머니와 매우 닮았다.
4. 그녀는 중간키입니다.
5. 그녀는 데뷔 영화 동안에는 날씬했다.
6. 나는 약간 과체중이다.
7. 그는 튼튼하고 근육질의 남자입니다.
8. 반수의 노인은 이들 약을 복용합니다.
9. 열 중 셋의 청년은 과음합니다.
10. 중년의 남자가 배회하는 것이 보인다.

Answer

01. plain
02. weighs
03. like
04. height
05. thin
06. overweight
07. muscular
08. elderly
09. youths
10. middle

※ 적절한 것을 골라 써넣으시오.

gain, looks, stands, weighs

1. pound → weigh/ weight
2. feet, inches → stand, height
3. tend to (하는 경향이다), gain/put on weight, lose/shed weight
4. resemble(= look like)
5. 지방(fat)과 근육
6. 키/높이
7. child/youth(청년)/ adult, childhood/youth(청년기)/ adulthood
8. 39/younger → age

01 Oprah says she ________ 200 pounds.

02 He ________ 6-feet, 6-inches and is still growing.

03 Women tend to ________ weight after they get married.

04 The baby ________ just like me. I feel like I'm looking in a mirror.

※ 적절한 것을 골라 써넣으시오.

age, height, muscle, youth

05 Build ________ and lose fat!

06 I want to know what is the right weight for my ________.

07 ________ is the time of life between childhood and adulthood.

08 Black, 39, is a sheet metal worker. He looks younger than his ________.

Answer

01. weighs
02. stands
03. gain
04. looks
05. muscle
06. height
07. Youth
08. age

※ 적절한 것을 골라 써넣으시오.

elderly, gorgeous, middle-aged, overweight

01 Many Americans are considered ________ or obese.

02 You look different, you look ________, I love kissing with you!

03 By 40, I felt I had no choice but to accept myself as being ________.

04 Rock Island family is collecting gifts and necessities for the ________ and poor.

1. obese (비만의), obesity (비만)
2. gorgeous(= very beautiful)
3. 40세 → 중년. 인정하다(accept), 부인하다 (deny)
4. necessities(생활필수품) ≠ conveniences(편의용품) elderly(= old; aged)
5. tall/medium/short
6. 노년층(the elderly; seniors)
7. nerve → nervous, caution → cautious, put on ≠ take off
8. 체중(weight), 신장(height), common ≠ uncommon

※ 반대 또는 대조되는 단어를 써넣으시오.

05 Is your boss **taller** or **s**________ than you?

06 The **youth** and the **e**________ today have many similarities.

07 I'm nervous about how to **put on** or **t**________ off my contact lenses.

08 'What is the right **weight** for my **h**________?' is one of the most common questions girls and guys have.

Answer

01. overweight
02. gorgeous
03. middle-aged
04. elderly
05. shorter
06. elderly
07. take
08. height

※ 괄호에 적절한 것을 고르시오.

1. alike(닮은),
   like(~와 닮은)
2. fit(= healthy),
   tin(깡통),
   thin(=slim)
3. either(= too),
   short/medium/tall
4. eat too much → fat
   (= overweight)
5. skinny(=too thin),
   gain weight ≠ lose weight
6. far from(= never),
   plain(평야; 못생긴)
7. age
8. weight
9. height
10. age
11. build(체격),
    character(성격)
12. plain(= homely)

01 What does she look (alike, like)?

02 I am a fit girl, not a (tin, thin) girl.

03 My nephew is not tall, but not short, either. He is (medium, middle) height.

04 My uncle is (overweight, underweight). He eats too much. He must go on a diet.

05 Andy is too (skinny, obese). He may want to gain weight.

06 She is far from (pretty, plain). She has beautiful eyes and a nice smile.

※ 관련 없는 하나의 단어에 X표 하시오.

07 aged, poor, elderly, old, senior

08 generous, lean, obese, slim, thin

09 average, medium, obese, short, tall

10 aging, serious, junior, little, young

11 age, build, character, height, weight

12 cute, plain, fashionable, lovely, stylish

Answer

01. like
02. thin
03. medium
04. overweight
05. skinny
06. plain
07. poor
08. generous
09. obese
10. serious
11. character
12. plain

※ 괄호에 적절한 단어를 고르시오.

01 Women (on, in) Black is a women's anti-war movement with an estimated 10,000 activists around the world.

02 The (older, elderly) and the youth are noticeably bad drivers, horrible even. Their driving capabilities are almost to the point where it should be a crime, but neither group would ever dare to admit to it.

03 I'm having trouble getting my 4-year-old daughter dressed in the morning. She has a lot of nice hand-me-downs — all in good condition — but she only wants to (ware, wear) the same jeans and the same shirt every day.

04 Not everyone grows and develops on the same schedule, but most people go through a period of faster growth during their teens. During puberty, the body begins making hormones that spark physical changes like faster muscle growth and spurts in height. As the amount of muscle, fat, and bone in the body changes during this time, some people might gain (height, weight) more rapidly.

1. in(= wearing),
   anti-war(전쟁을 반대하는)
2. noticeably(뜨일 정도로),
   horrible (=very bad),
   dare(감히 ~하다),
   admit ≠refuse
3. trouble(= difficulty),
   in good condition(상태가 양호한),
4. a period of faster growth
   → puberty → this time,
   rapidly(= fast)

Answer

01. in
02. elderly
03. wear
04. weight

② The woman in black

※ 옷(clothes, clothing, wear, costume), casual **wear**, Santa **costume**
get dressed up
≠ dress casually,
She looks good **in** almost everything.

외모를 입은 옷, 헤어스타일로 묘사하기도 한다. 옛날에 옷은 주로 여자가 만들어서인지, 남녀 구분 없이 옷 입다 → dress; get dressed

★ **Get dressed** up for work.

★ Look at the woman **in** black.

※ make-up(화장),
wear(= put on)
≠ take/strip off,
imitation(= fake),
fur (모피),
strip/stripped/stripped

장신구/화장/신발을 착용하거나 벗을 때도

Put on your earrings and make-up.

★ She **wears** an imitation fur coat.

★ Please **take off** your shoes.

He **stripped off** his shirt.

※ take down ≠ pull up,
button ≠ unbutton,
skinny(= very tight)

바지/치마를 내리거나 올릴 때, 단추나 지프를 채울 때, 크기를 맞출 때

★ **Take down** your pants and bend over.

★ Don't forget to **zip up** your pants.

★ **Button up** your jacket.

Nicky wears **skinny** jeans.

※ buy/bought/bought, 줄(striped)/꽃(floral; flowery)/체크(checked) / 물방울(spotted) / 땡땡이(dotted)

옷의 무늬가 줄/꽃/체크/물방울/땡땡이

★ She bought me a **striped** shirt.

Wear this **floral** dress with the cardigan.

※ long/medium/short,
shoulder/waist/knee/floor length, round (둥근),
thin (가냘픈), oval (달걀형),
straight(직모)/wavy(파상)/curly(곱슬),
wave → wavy

머리가 길고/중간/짧고, 직모/파상/곱슬이거나, 얼굴이 가냘픈/둥근/달걀형일 수 있다.

★ My hair is **shoulder length**.

★ I have a **round** face and **wavy** hair.

※ 빈칸에 적절한 단어를 써 넣으시오.

01 Don't forget to zip **u**__________ your pants.

02 **B**__________ up your jacket while standing.

03 She bought me a zebra-**s**__________ shirt.

04 Take **d**__________ your pants and bend over.

05 Please **t**__________ off your shoes before you come inside.

06 She **w**__________ an imitation fur coat. It appears to be real fur.

07 My hair is shoulder **l**__________. It is not too long, not too short.

08 Look at the woman **i**__________ black. She lost her husband in the car accident.

09 I have a round face and naturally **w**__________ hair. My hair is neither straight nor curly.

10 Do you prefer a profession where you can get dressed **u**__________ for work or dress casually?

1. 바지 지퍼를 잊지 말고 올려.
2. 자켓의 단추를 채우세요.
3. 그녀는 나에게 줄무늬 셔츠를 사주었다.
4. 바지 내리고 구부려.
5. 신을 벗으세요.
6. 그녀는 인조 모피 코트를 입고 있다.
7. 내 머리는 어깨 길이입니다.
8. 검은 옷 입은 여자 분을 보세요.
9. 나는 둥근 얼굴과 파상형 머리를 가졌어요.
10. 일할 때 정장 입는 직장 또는 비정장을 입는 직장을 선호하세요.

Answer

01. up
02. Button
03. striped
04. down
05. take
06. wears
07. length
08. in
09. wavy
10. up

※ 적절한 동사를 골라 써넣으시오.

button, put, strip, wear

1. school uniform(교복)
2. suit jacket(정장상의), while standing
   → while you stand
3. take off(벗다), strip off(홀랑 벗다)
4. take off/pull off /strip off (=remove), put on/have on(=wear)
5. wary(=careful; watchful)
6. take or leave, off ≠ on
7. 매 맞으려면(spanking) 바지를? take down/pull down/ get down(내리다). Bare bottomed, I'd be spanked long and hard.
8. He forgot to zip up his pants.
9. put on/pull on/try on, eye(눈여겨두다)

01 Should students __________ school uniforms?

02 Please __________ up your suit jacket while standing.

03 We saw this guy __________ off his shirt and jump into the water.

04 I need to change my clothes. I'll take off my suit and __________ on some jeans.

※ 적절한 것을 골라 써넣으시오.

down, in, off, on, up

05 Be wary of the woman __________ red.

06 You can either take __________ your hat or leave your hat on.

07 Did any of you have to pull your pants __________ for a spanking?

08 How do you tell someone that he needs to zip his pants __________?

09 I tried __________ my wedding dress.

I eyed the dress for months.

Answer

01. wear
02. button
03. strip
04. change
05. in
06. off
07. down
08. up
09. on

※ 관련 없는 하나의 단어에 X표 하시오.

01 blond, brown, gray, starry, white

02 big, large, huge, over-sized, tiny

03 fat, overweight, plump, slender, stout

04 reasonable, inexpensive, costly, rash

05 lazy, curly, red-haired, straight, wavy

1. color 관련. star → starry
2. tiny(= very small)
3. slender(= slim; thin), stout(통통한)
4. price 관련. rash(성급한)
5. hair 관련. lazy(≠ diligent)
6. pull up(당겨 올리다), outfit(겉옷)
7. knee length (무릎 높이의), floor length (바닥 닿는)
8. woman/women
9. dress shoes (정장 구두), formal ≠ casual
10. The width of the face is about the same as its length.

※ 괄호에 적절한 것을 고르시오.

06 She pulled up her skirt. She wasn't wearing any (underwear, outfit).

07 My parents don't let me wear pants and I have to wear a knee (long, length) skirt.

08 They shop women's shoes, boots and sandals at the (footwear, costume) store.

09 All men in the office should wear pants with a belt and a (casual, dress) shirt.

10 If you have a face that is as long as it's wide, then you have a (round, square) face.

Answer

01. starry
02. tiny
03. slender
04. rash
05. lazy
06. underwear
07. length
08. footwear
09. dress
10. square

※ 무늬의 이름을 골라 써넣으시오.

checked, flowery, spotted, striped

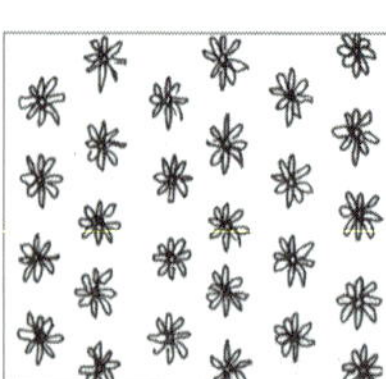

01 ________

02 ________

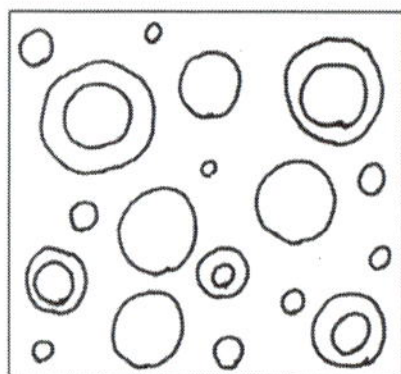

03 ________

04 ________

※ 적절한 그림을 고르시오.

05 a crew-cut ________

06 round-faced with wavy hair ________

07 thin-faced with straight hair ________

08 dark-skinned with curly hair ________

(A)

(B)

(C)

(D)

1. 꽃의(= flowery; floral), florist(꽃집주인), floral dresses; floral wallpaper
2. the Stars and Stripes (성조기), a white shirt with a thin grey stripe
3. 점 (spot), a red and white spotted handkerchief
4. a checked blouse, a checkerboard floor,
5. crew-cut(= buzz cut),
6. round ≠ thin, wavy ≠ straight
8. dark ≠ light, curly(곱슬한)

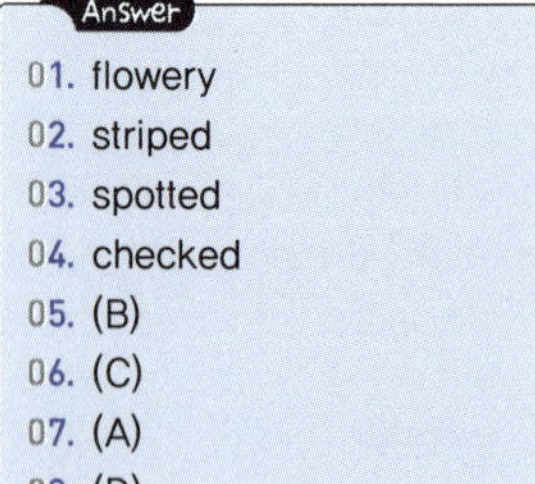

Answer

01. flowery
02. striped
03. spotted
04. checked
05. (B)
06. (C)
07. (A)
08. (D)

※ 빈칸에 적절한 단어를 써넣으시오.

01 How can I never forget to **z**__________ up **my fly** and make a fool of myself while I give a presentation in front of the class?

02 "Starting from being naked, what order do you get dressed in?" "For me, it goes : brief, bra, **j**______, **t-shirt**, jewelry, socks, hair and makeup. And you?"

03 There are two types of weight **l**__________: intentional and unintentional. When a person intentionally **loses weight**, he typically plans a diet and/or exercise program designed to lose a certain amount of pounds over a set period of time.

04 People judge others by the **a**__________ of the outside. It is a sad fact but it is true. Special people are missed because they aren't the most attractive people and sometimes a person who **appears** to be a model may really be disagreeable but overlooked because of the "pretty" factor.

1. fly(= clothes; outfit), make a fool of(조롱하다)
2. naked(= bare; nude), get dressed(옷 입다), in what order(어떤 순서로), makeup(화장)
3. weigh/weight, lose/ loss, intentionally(= on purpose; purposely), a set period of time(정해진 기간)
4. appearance(= look, 외모), attractive(= good-looking), disagreeable(= 불쾌한, obnoxious), overlook(간과하다), because of(= owing to; due to)

Answer

01. zip
02. jeans
03. loss
04. appearance

※ 관계없는 하나의 단어에 X표 하시오.

01 slim, thin, slender, skinny, obese

02 blouse, shirt, jeans, jacket, sweater

03 pretty, plain, beautiful, attractive, cute

04 pants, slacks, shorts, gloves, trousers

05 cuffs, shoes, sneakers, boots, sandals

※ 괄호에 적절한 단어를 고르시오.

06 This life-size poster of Jacob stands 6 feet (tall, high).

07 All my shoes are arranged in (lows, rows) on the floor.

08 She is a little (pet, fat), but she has a beautiful face and a divine voice.

09 Bob came dressed (casually, formally) in tennis shoes, a T-shirt and running shorts.

10 My new jacket needs to be (altered, exchanged). Please have the sleeves shortened and the lapels made narrower.

1. obese(= very fat), skin → skinny, bone → bony, hair → hairy
2. upper clothing
3. plain(= homely), attractive(= good-looking)
4. clothes for the lower body, gloves(장갑), mittens(벙어리장갑)
5. footwear
6. life-size(실물크기)
7. arranged(정돈된), row (줄)
8. pet (애완동물), divine(신성한)
9. casually (비정장으로)
10. alter(= change), exchange(교환하다), shortened(짧게 된), made narrower(좁게 된)

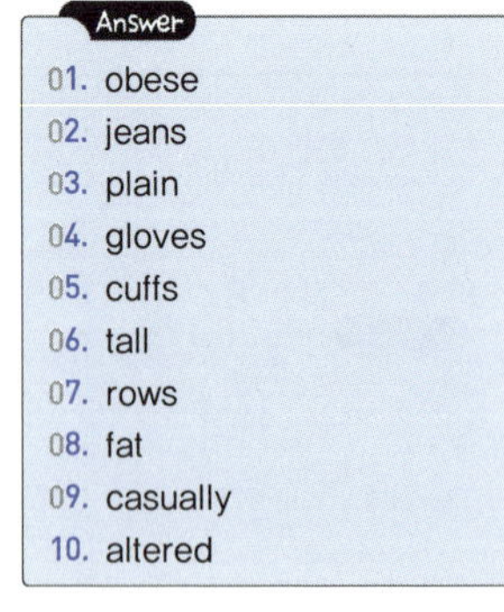

Answer

01. obese
02. jeans
03. plain
04. gloves
05. cuffs
06. tall
07. rows
08. fat
09. casually
10. altered

exercise 4

※적절한 동의어를 써넣으시오.

01 a slim finger = s________

02 shed weight = l________

03 flowery design = f________

04 put on your shirt = w________

05 an overweight guy = f________

06 You are well-built. = m________

07 a good-looking guy = a________

08 look very beautiful = g________

09 a shirt with stripes = s________

10 some young persons = y________

11 to wear a dress shirt = f________

12 to look like his father = r________

1. thin
2. ≠ gain
3. florist
4. ≠ take off
5. ≠ underweight
6. muscle의 형용사
7. 매력적
8. 매우 예쁜
9. 줄무늬의
10. 젊은이
11. not casual
12. 닮다
13. curly ≠ straight
14. zebra(얼룩말), strip/stripped/stripped

※ 괄호에 적절한 것을 고르시오.

13 Make curly hair (straight, straightly).

14 She is wearing a zebra (stripped, striped) shirt.

15. likely(= probable), gain/lose weight
16. are supposed to (= should)
17. loose ≠ tight
18. chase(추적)
19. insist(고집하다)
20. tall(= in height)

15 Women are more likely to gain (weigh, weight) after marriage.

16 You are supposed to (button, unbutton) your jacket when you sit.

17 Some people actually prefer (lose, loose) clothes to tight ones.

18 I saw the man (in, on) black running through the town, so I gave chase.

19 My hairdresser insists that my hair is waist (long, length).

20 The average (tall, height) in Korea is 174cm for men and 161 for women.

My grade : ________/20

Test 4

ID :   Name :

※ 주어진 단어를 사용하여 영어로 옮기시오.

01 그녀는 중간키입니다. (medium height)

____

02 그녀는 영리하고 날씬하고 아름다운 여자다. (smart slim)

____

03 그녀는 예쁜가요, 못생겼나요? (pretty, plain)

____

04 중년의 남자가 배회하는 것이 보인다. (wandering around)

____

05 반수의 노인은 이 약을 먹습니다. (the elderly, these drugs)

____

06 직장 갈 때 정장을 입으세요. (for work)

____

07 검은 옷 입은 여자를 보세요. (look at)

____

08 재킷의 단추를 채우세요. (button)

____

09 그녀는 나에게 줄무늬 셔츠를 사 주었다. (striped)

____

10 나는 둥근 얼굴과 파상형 머리를 가졌어요. (round, wavy)

____

My grade : ______/10

Unit

05

Give me the recipe

Unit.

05 Give me the recipe

1 Chop the onion

요리법(recipe)에 따라 식재료를 잘게 썰고, 갈고, 양념하고.

★ **Chop** the onions into small pieces.

★ **Grind** the beef to flatten into patties.

★ **Season** with salt and pepper.

★ Ask me some vegetarian **recipes**.

※ chop(= cut, 잘게 썰다)
grind(= mince, 갈다),
ground beef(갈아놓은 쇠고기),
season(양념하다),
양념(seasoning) : herbs/spices/salt/soy sauce,
vegetarian(채식주의자)

불을 가하여 데우고/굽고/프라이하면,

★ How long should I **heat** tomato soup?

I'd like to learn how to **bake** muffins.

★ **Grill** the chicken pieces.

Eggs are easy to **fry** or **scramble**.

※ heat(= warm up, 데우다),
boil(삶다),
bake bread(빵을 굽다),
grill(야외에서 굽다),
chicken pieces(= breasts, legs, thighs, wings),
scramble(휘저어 익히다)

'먹다/씹다/삼키다/핥아먹다'도 잘 아시죠.

★ **Chew** your food well.

Don't spit. **Swallow**.

★ **Lick** an ice cream.

Consume yogurt before its expiration date.

※ eat(= have, 먹다),
chew(씹다),
swallow(제비; 삼키다),
lick(= lap, 핥아먹다),
spit(침 뱉다),
consume(= eat or drink),
expire(만료되다),
expiration(만료)

※ silverware/dinnerware
plate(접시),
platter(쟁반),
bowl(사발),
glass/plastic/wooden / metal bowl

folk/knife/plates/bowls 등을 tableware라고

Use a **fork** and **knife** properly.

★ Can you fix a broken **plate**?

★ Serve potato salad in a **bowl**.

〈수량형용사〉

1. 셀 수 있는/없는 명사에 모두 쓸 수 있는 수량형용사
   some tips/some advice, **any** letters/any mail, **other** lakes/other water, **enough** dollars/enough money, **plenty of** facts/plenty of information,
   a lot of jobs/a lot of work, **all** chairs/all furniture

2. 셀 수 있는/없는 명사 어느 한쪽 앞에만 쓸 수 있는 수량형용사
   a bag, few bags, **little** baggage/ an hour, a few hours, **a little** time/ another tool, various tools, several tools, **much** equipment/ every dress, many dresses, a number of dresses, **a great deal of** clothing

※ 괄호에 적절한 것을 고르시오.
1. Do you need (a, lots of) job?
2. Do you have a lot of (bag, baggage)?
3. I'd like (other, another) slice of cake
4. The factory hired (another, all the) men.
5. He gave me several safety (tips, advice).
6. Eligon has stayed busy with the store open at (all, every) hours.
7. Do you have enough (fact, information) to make a good decision?

Answers
1. a 2. baggage 3. another 4. all the 5. tips 6. all 7. information

※ 빈칸에 적절한 단어를 써 넣으시오.

01 **S**__________ with salt and pepper.

02 **G**__________ the beef to flatten into patties.

03 Is it okay to make and serve potato salad in a metal **b**__________?

04 **L**__________ an ice cream but not bite or chew it.

05 Let's **g**__________ the chicken pieces over an open fire.

06 **C**__________ your food well because that will help your digestion.

07 I want to cook tomato soup. How long should I **h**__________ the soup?

08 **C**__________ the onions, running your knife through them in a rocking motion.

09 Is it possible to repair cracked bone china? Can you fix a broken **p**__________?

10 Would you like to prepare vegetarian dishes? Ask me some vegetarian **r**__________.

1. 소금과 후추로 양념해요.
2. 쇠고기를 갈아 납작하게 패티로 만드시오.
3. 금속의 사발.
   I know metal contaminates some foods, but would this be safe?
4. 아이스크림을 핥아 먹어.
5. 닭고기 조각을 야외 불 위에 구웁시다.
6. 음식을 잘 씹으시오.
7. 토마토 수프를 얼마나 오랫동안 데워야 하나요?
8. 양파를 잘게 써시오.
9. 깨어진 접시를 수리할 수 있나요?
10. 나에게 몇 가지 채식주의 요리법을 요청하세요.

Answer

01. Season
02. Grind
03. bowl
04. Lick
05. grill
06. Chew
07. heat
08. Chop
09. plate
10. recipes

※ 적절한 동사를 골라 써넣으시오.

chew, chop, grind, lick

1. bite, chew하는 분도 있지만 주로 핥아먹는다
2. 씹는 껌 (chewing gum)
3. grind/ground/ground ground beef/pepper(갈은 쇠고기/후추)
4. cut into small pieces. some … others에 유의.
5. 튀기다. place(= put)
6. 석쇠(grated utensil)에 굽다
7. 마르지(dry) 않도록 기름을 발라?
8. boil eggs

01 __________ your ice cream slowly.

02 __________ your food long enough for your stomach to feel full.

03 __________ the beef with a food processor to make hamburger patties.

04 __________ vegetables without leaving some pieces bigger than others.

※ 적절한 동사를 골라 써넣으시오.

boil, fry, grill, roast

05 __________ to cook by placing in hot oil

06 __________ to broil meat using a grated utensil

07 __________ to cook meat using a little oil on it

08 __________ to cook by placing food in hot water

Answer

01. Lick
02. Chew
03. Grind
04. Chop
05. fry
06. grill
07. roast
08. boil

※ 적절한 명사를 골라 써넣으시오.

bowl, plates, recipe, saucer

01 "I am drinking from my __________ cause my cup overflows."

02 These apple pies are so delicious. You must give me the __________.

03 Cut the cherry tomatoes in half and place in a large salad __________.

04 I love these __________. They're Limoges china with a little lemon motif on them.

1. room and board, mug and coaster, cup and saucer
2. delicious(= tasty), how to cook(= recipe)
3. cut in half(반쪽으로 자르다), place(= put), salad dressing/oil/bowl
4. china(= cups, plates, saucers, dishes, etc.)
5. ways to eat
6. chop(= cut into pieces)
7. consume(= eat or drink)
8. peeler(껍질 벗기는 도구), cooker(주방기구)
9. flour (밀가루), flower (꽃)
10. heat(= warm up)

※ 관계없는 하나의 단어에 X표 하시오.

05 bite, grill, chew, lick, swallow

06 bake, boil, broil, chop, fry, stew

07 consume, drink, eat, have, purchase

08 chef, cooker, pan, peeler, toaster

09 chocolate, pie, cake, fork, cookies

10 cut, chop, grind, mince, heat

Answer

01. saucer
02. recipe
03. bowl
04. plates
05. grill
06. chop
07. purchase
08. chef
09. fork
10. heat

※ 반대 또는 대조되는 단어를 써넣으시오.

1. 후추
2. local ≠ national, 버터를 어디에 발라 먹지?
3. 조리기구
4. specialty shop(전문점), carry(취급하다), a variety of(= various)
5. tea pot (차 주전자), sugar and cream, cup and saucer, mug and coaster
6. drop out of(= quit, 자퇴하다), as long as(= if), is quitting(그만 둘 것이다), full time ≠ part time, gross income(총소득), net income(순소득)

01 Pass me the **salt** and **p**__________.

02 Teaching at the local college is his **b**__________ and **butter**.

03 Kevin keeps his **pots** and **p**__________ in the cabinet below the stove.

04 Oil and **vinegar** specialty shops carry a variety of fruit vinegars that would work well in this **s**__________.

05 The tea pot itself is only $9.99 and the sugar and cream holders are $4.99 each. Each **cup** and **s**__________ is $6.99.

06 My son is almost 19. He is dropping out of college near the end of his freshman year. He was told that as long as he was in school, he'd not be charged **room** and **b**__________. Now he is quitting school, has a job at $8.50 an hour cooking for a steakhouse and working full time. That's about $340 a week gross, about $272 net, and about $1088 a month net.

Answer

01. pepper
02. bread
03. pans
04. salad
05. saucer
06. board

※ 괄호에 적절한 것을 고르시오.

01 (Heat, Hot) the soup in the pan and stir it.

02 Chew your food well and (swell, swallow) it.

03 (Scatter, Season) with salt, pepper, and two or three light gratings of nutmeg.

04 You can (fry, scramble) eggs directly in the pan by cracking the eggs then stirring.

05 (Chip, Chop) or crush the walnuts as finely as you can. If you haven't been able to get ground cardomum you will have to bash some in their pods and (grind, ground) the seeds yourself.

06 But I was sick and (tired, hungry) all the time. I went to churches and food banks and barely survived on expired and (rot, rotten) food. Peanut butter, pasta, rice and tuna is not exactly a balanced diet. I had no fresh produce except at one food bank.

1. warm up(= heat), stir(= mix)
2. swell(= expand), swallow(삼키다),
3. scatter(흩다), season(양념하다)
4. crack(= break), stir(= mix)
5. crush(짓이기다), finely ≠ coarsely, pod(콩의 꼬투리), grind/ground/ground, seeds(씨, 종자)
6. all the time(= always), barely(간신히), expired(만료된), produce(채소 및 과일)

Answer

01. Heat
02. swallow
03. Season
04. scramble
05. Chop, grind
06. hungry, rotten

② An imaginative cook

✷ cook(요리사), chef(주방장), 주방기구 : oven, barbecue grill, slow cooker 등

요리사를 영어로? cook? cooker?

★ She is an imaginative **cook**.

★ I do bulgogi in my slow **cooker**.

✷ **food** : meat/vegetables / fish/seafood, prefer(= like better), **beverage** : tea, coffee, soda, cider(= apple juice), **meals** : breakfast, lunch, brunch, dinner **refreshments** : food and beverage

음식(food), 음료수(beverage), 식사 (meals)

★ I prefer **meat** and **seafood**.

★ Milk is the only **beverage** we have.

We have three **meals** a day.

★ **Refreshments** are now being served.

★ Coffee in the morning **smells good**.

✷ favorite(= preferred; preference), familiar with(= knowing well), ethnic(민족의), concerned(= worried; anxious), safe → safety, cruel → cruelty

후식(dessert)에는 cookies, fruit, pies, ice cream 등이 있다. 민족음식(ethnic food), 식품안전(food safety)

★ Ice cream is my favorite **dessert**.

★ Apple pies **taste sweet**.

★ He is familiar with **ethnic food**.

★ I'm concerned about **food safety**.

※ 빈칸에 적절한 단어를 써 넣으시오.

01 Apple pies **t**__________ **sweet**.

02 I do bulgogi in my slow **c**__________.

03 I prefer meat and **s**__________ to fruits and vegetables.

04 Ice cream is my favorite **d**__________ in every season.

05 She is an imaginative **c**__________. She makes chef's salads.

06 Light **r**__________ are now being served : coffee and doughnuts.

07 No tea, coffee, beer, and soda. Milk is the only **b**__________ we have.

08 Coffee in the morning **s**__________ **good**. The aroma makes me full of joy.

09 He is familiar with **e**__________ **food** : Chinese, Vietnamese, Mexican, and more.

10 How safe is the food you purchase?
I'm concerned about **food** **s**__________.

1. 사과파이는 맛이 달다.
2. 나는 슬로쿠커로 불고기를 합니다.
3. 나는 육류와 해산물을 선호한다.
4. 내가 가장 좋아하는 디저트는 아이스크림 이다.
5. 그녀는 창의적 요리사 다.
6. 지금 다과류가 제공됩니다.
7. 사과주스는 우리가 가진 유일한 음료수이다.
8. 아침의 커피는 냄새가 좋다.
9. 그는 민족 음식을 잘 안다.
10. 식품 안전을 우려하세요?

Answer

01. taste
02. cooker
03. seafood
04. dessert
05. cook
06. Refreshments
07. beverage
08. smells
09. ethnic
10. safety

※ 적절한 것을 골라 써넣으시오.

dessert, drink, seafood, vegetables

1. during my pregnancy (= while I'm pregnant)
2. crab(게), lobster(가재), oyster(굴)
3. apple pie, pudding 등 → dessert
4. cucumber(오이), fruits or veggies
5. on ≠ off, 전기압력조리기구
6. taste(= flavor)
7. food and drink, at(시각), on(날짜), in(달/연도)
8. consume(= eat or drink), coffee, water → beverages(= drinks)

01 Is it safe to have a __________ or two at dinner during my pregnancy?

02 We may eat fish, sushi, crab, lobster, oyster at a __________ restaurant.

03 I was glad to see apple pie, pudding, fruit and ice cream as __________.

04 I like pumpkins, tomatoes and cucumbers. Are they fruits or __________?

※ 적절한 것을 골라 써넣으시오.

beverage, cooker, flavors, refreshments

05 She switched on an electric pressure __________.

06 The ice cream comes in three __________: strawberry, chocolate and vanilla.

07 Light __________ will be served at 6:45. The meeting will begin at 7:00.

08 Coffee is the second most consumed __________ on the planet after water.

Answer
01. drink
02. seafood
03. dessert
04. vegetables
05. cooker
06. flavors
07. refreshments
08. beverage

※ 괄호에 적절한 것을 고르시오.

01 Would you like something to (drink, beverage)?

02 In general, men prefer (meat, meet) and poultry while women prefer fruits and vegetables.

03 How do I know if this is (safe, safety) to eat? Is there something in this food that could make me sick?

04 Kelly assisted his mother, a restaurant chef, while his father was a railroad (cook, cooker) on the Illinois Central.

1. 마실 어떤 것?
2. 남자(a man; men; gentlemen), 여자(a woman; women; ladies), prefer(선호하다) → preference … poultry (가금류), but(= while; whereas, 반면에)
3. be 동사 아래에 형용사
4. assist(= help), while(= whereas; but)
5. interested in; involved in
6. suspicious of; doubtful of; dubious of
7. knowing well (= familiar with)
8. concerned about; worried about
9. from … to/until/ through …

※ 적절한 전치사를 써넣으시오.

05 I am not interested ________ food.

06 I'm doubtful ________ its freshness.

07 She is familiar ________ Chinese food.

08 The Chinese are increasingly concerned ________ the foods they eat.

09 Our restaurant is open 11:00AM to 9:00PM Wednesday ________ Monday.

Answer
01. drink
02. meat
03. safe
04. cook
05. in
06. of
07. with
08. about
09. through

※ 괄호에 적절한 것을 고르시오.

01 The rotten meat smells (bad, fragrant).

02 Why do chili peppers taste (hot, cool)?

03 "What (ethnic, popular) food have you tried?"
"I like most Asian dishes."

04 (Raw, Cooked) fish is sashimi and is often used as a topping for sushi.

05 By the time I had finished talking on the phone my food was (warm, lukewarm).

※ 토픽에 해당하는 단어에 O표 하시오.

06 chicken/lamb/meat/pork/steak

07 celery/lettuce/vegetable/radish

08 baguette/bread/bun/muffin/roll

09 fork/silverware/knife/ladle/spoon

10 beverage/coke/juice/lemonade/milk

11 cake/cookies/dessert/ice cream/pie

1. rotten(=decayed), fragrant (=sweet-smelling)
2. chili vs. chilly
3. Japanese, Chinese, Thai, Vietnamese and so on.
4. raw(=uncooked)
5. lukewarm(=slightly warm; tepid)
6. lamb(새끼 양; 양고기)
7. lettuce(양상추), radish(무)
8. roll (동그란 빵), a roll and butter, a dozen rolls
9. ladle (국자), I ladle the soup into bowls.
10. drinks
11. sweets

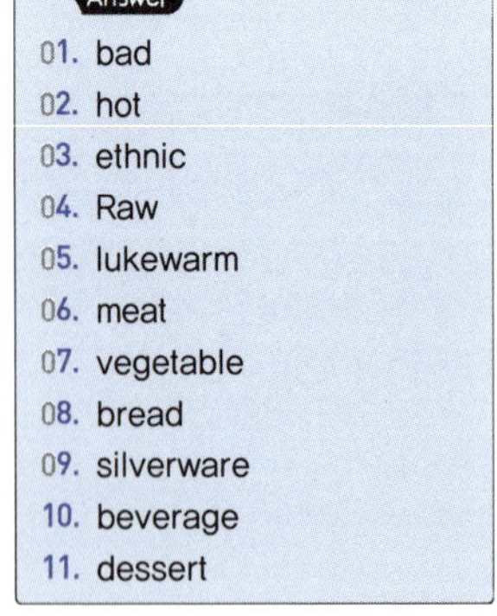
Answer
01. bad
02. hot
03. ethnic
04. Raw
05. lukewarm
06. meat
07. vegetable
08. bread
09. silverware
10. beverage
11. dessert

※ 괄호에 적절한 단어를 고르시오.

01 A (saucer, platter) goes under a cup.

02 Last night we ate (flesh, fresh) fish with corn and rice for dinner.

03 Mom's apple pie is the perfect afternoon snack or (desert, dessert).

04 (Keep, Stop) snacking on cookies and crackers. Dinner will be in an hour.

05 We won't need plates. This soup will be the whole meal. We'll only need (balls, bowls).

1. platter (쟁반), cup and saucer, mug and coaster
2. flesh (살코기), fresh ≠ rotten
3. snack(간식), dessert(후식)
4. snack(군것질하다), in an hour(한 시간 후)
5. won't(= will not), plates(접시), soup in the bowl
6. 그릇이 아닌 것?
7. no flour
8. cooking과 관련 없는?
9. 우유와 관련 없는?
10. lettuce (양상추)
11. faucet (수도꼭지)

※ 관계없는 하나의 단어에 X표 하시오.

06 cup, glass, straw, mug, bowl

07 cake, cookies, bread, salad, pie

08 cook, pot, pan, carpenter, stove

09 butter, cheese, milk, sugar, cream

10 chicken, pork, lamb, lettuce, rabbit

11 faucet, fork, knife, spoon, silverware

Answer

01. saucer
02. fresh
03. dessert
04. Stop
05. bowls
06. straw
07. salad
08. carpenter
09. sugar
10. lettuce
11. faucet

※ 빈칸에 적절한 단어를 써넣으시오.

1. 음료수 (drink; beverage)
2. chef(주방장), cook(요리사), oversee(= supervise), direct(지시하다), handle(= deal with)
3. identify(확인하다), till date (=up to now; so far), approximately(= roughly), vary(= differ; be different), attribute(속성), like(= such as), flesh(고기, 과육)
4. sorts(=kinds), fresh ≠ rotten

01 Would you like **tea, coffee, beer, milk** or any other **b**__________?

02 **Chefs** and head **c**__________ oversee the daily food preparation at restaurants or other places where food is served. They direct kitchen staff and handle any food-related concerns.

03 How many types of apples are identified till date? Believe it or not, there are approximately 7,500 **different** types of apples. They **v**__________ in specific attributes, like taste, skin color, flesh texture, flavor and uses.

04 The supermarket has special sections for different sorts of foods. **Milk, yogurt, and cheese** are kept in the **d**__________ section. Chicken, pork and beef are kept in the meat section. Fresh **fruits and vegetables** are kept in the **p**__________ section.

Answer

01. beverage
02. cooks
03. vary
04. dairy, produce

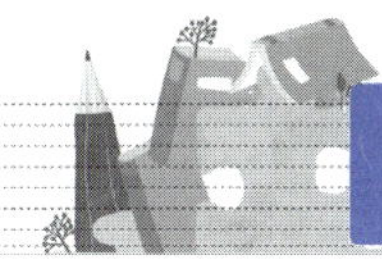

exercise 5

※ 적절한 동의어를 써넣으시오.

01 to mince beef = g________

02 to eat or drink = c________

03 strawberry flavor = t________

04 to eat fish raw = u________

05 food and beverage = r________

06 beverages available = d________

07 to warm up the soup = h________

08 fish, crab, oyster etc = s________

09 to broil chicken pieces = g________

10 concerned about safety = w________

1. 갈다
2. 섭취하다
3. 맛; 향
4. 날 것의
5. 다과
6. 음료수
7. 데우다
8. 해산물
9. 야외에서 굽다
10. 걱정하는
11. 사발
12. grind/ground /ground
13. 요리사 (cook; chef)
14. vinegar (식초)
15. knowing well

※ 괄호에 적절한 것을 고르시오.

11 Pass me the salad (ball, bowl).

12 (Grind, Ground) your own beef.

13 She is a fantastic (cook, cooker).

14 Hops and vinegar taste (bitter, sweet).

15 I'm familiar (to, with) Vietnamese food.

16. 양념하다
17. peel(껍질 벗기다), peeler(껍질 벗기는 도구), chop(잘게 썰다)
18. slow cooker(조리기구의 일종)
19. trash(= garbage)
20. besides (제외하고)

16 (Season, Shake) it with salt and pepper.

17 Peel a garlic clove and (chew, chop) it into thin slices.

18 This (recipe, spice) starts with onions in a slow cooker.

19 Trash cans can smell (bad, good) when you don't clean and maintain them.

20 What are your favorite (deserts, desserts) besides cookies and brownies?

My grade : ________ /20

Test 5

ID :　　　　　　　Name :

※ 주어진 단어를 사용하여 영어로 옮기시오.

01 양파를 잘게 써시오. (into small pieces)

____

02 소고기를 가시오. (grind)

____

03 얼마나 오랫동안 토마토 수프를 데워야 하나요? (heat)

____

04 음식을 잘 씹으시오. (chew)

____

05 깨어진 접시를 수리할 수 있나요? (fix)

____

06 그녀는 창의적 요리사다. (imaginative)

____

07 나는 채소보다 육류를 선호한다. (prefer… to …)

____

08 우유는 우리가 가진 유일한 음료수이다. (beverage)

___

09 사과 파이는 맛이 달다. (sweet)

___

10 그는 민족음식을 잘 안다. (familiar)

___

My grade : ______/10

Unit

06

Have a family

Unit.

06 Have a family

① Spell your family name

결혼신분(marital status)이 독신/약혼/결혼/이혼인가요?

Will you **marry** me?

★ I **got married** at the age of 24.

★ I **have a family** of four.

※ I'm single(독신의)/ engaged(약혼한)/ married(결혼한)/ divorced(이혼한)

성명을 주고받을 때 first name(Mike, Batty 등)은 금방 이해되지만, 상대방의 family name은 그렇지 못한 경우가 많다. 이때

How do you **spell** your family name?

※ 남자 : Bill, Chris, Jacob, Dan, Matty, Andy, 여자 : Emma, Sarah, Olivia, Sophia, Ella, Sue 등. spell → spelling (철자), a dry spell (건조한 시기),

신혼부부(newlyweds)는 남편과 아내의 역할을 가지며 집안잡일(chores)을 분담한다.

I **vacuum** the carpeted floors everyday.

★ You **did laundry** all morning.

※ 진공소제 하다(vacuum), 빨래하다(do laundry). (세탁물) : a **laundry** basket, (세탁소) : send it to the **laundry**, chores(= housework), do chores(집안잡일 하다)

각종 수리도 빠트릴 수 없으며, 간혹 가라지 세일(garage sale; yard sale)도 한다.

★ I **repaired** my chair.

★ We built a wine cellar in the **basement**.

★ Tools were sold at a **reasonable** price.

※ garage(차고, 자동차 수리소), repair(= fix; mend), basement(지하실), cheap/inexpensive/ **reasonable**/expensive

※ bring up(= raise),
in strict way(= strictly)
look after(= attend to : take care of),
graduate from(= leave),
invite → invitation(초대),
relative(친척)

부부의 sleep together/have sex/make love 는 출산과 자녀양육으로 연결

I want to **have a baby** and he doesn't.

★ We **bring up** our child in strict way.

★ I **looked after** my grandchildren.

★ He **graduated from** a college.

★ We invited **relatives** to his wedding.

1. Gone with the wind
2. 떠나다
3. have come
4. I got here by bus.
5. 기다
6. have run; is run
7. have done; is done
8. red과 발음동일
9. eight과 발음동일
10. drunken은 형용사
11. bring up children
12. tell a tale
13. written or spoken English

※ 원형/과거형/과거분사형을 써넣으시오.

#	원형	과거형	과거분사형
1	go	went	
2		left	left
3	come	came	
4	get		gotten
5		crept	crept
6	run	ran	
7	do	did	
8	read	read	
9	eat		eaten
10	drink	drank	
11		brought	brought
12		told	told
13	speak	spoke	

Answer

01. gone 02. leave
03. come 04. got
05. creep 06. run
07. done 08. read
09. ate 10. drunk
11. bring 12. tell
13. spoken

※ 빈칸에 적절한 단어를 써 넣으시오.

01 We **b**__________ up our children strictly.

02 Is it too early if someone wants to get **m**__________ at the age of 24?

03 I have a **f**__________ of four : husband, daughter, son and me.

04 I **r**__________ my chair yesterday. It looked new again!

05 Tools were sold at a **r**__________ price. Neither cheap nor expensive.

06 My son got married in May. We invited **r**__________ to his wedding.

07 I **l**__________ after my grandchildren while my daughter went out of town.

08 I did **l**__________ all morning and I still have more things to wash this afternoon!

09 How old was Martin Luther King jr when he graduated **f**__________ a college?

10 We built a wine cellar in the **b**__________ where we store wine and entertain guests.

1. 우리는 자녀를 엄격히 양육한다.
2. 24세에 결혼하다
3. 저는 4명의 가족을 가지고 있어요.
4. 나는 나의 의자를 수리했다.
5. 장비들은 적절한 가격에 팔렸다.
6. 우리는 그의 결혼식에 친척을 초대했다.
7. 나는 손자녀를 돌봤다.
8. 아침 내내 나는 빨래를 했다.
9. 그는 대학을 졸업했다. He was 26 years old.
10. 나는 지하실에 와인저장소를 만들었다.

Answer

01. bring
02. married
03. family
04. repaired
05. reasonable
06. relatives
07. looked
08. laundry
09. from
10. basement

※ 적절한 것을 골라 써넣으시오.

bring, divorced, graduated, married

01 William __________ from Harvard with a degree in Economics.

02 Chaerim and Lee Seung Hwan __________ after three years of marriage.

03 Most parents find it difficult to __________ up their children nowadays.

04 I am engaged to be __________ but my ex-boyfriend is blackmailing me.

※ 적절한 것을 골라 써넣으시오.

do, dust, fix, sweep

05 __________ your own furniture to save money.

06 Why don't you __________ the broken glass with a broom?

07 Love it or hate it, everyone has to __________ the laundry at some point.

08 __________ the blinds and then clean the floor with a mop and bucket.

1. degree(학사학위), leave school(= graduate from school)
2. marry ≠ divorce, marry → marriage
   engage → engagement
3. bring up(= raise)
4. 약혼(engaged) → 결혼(married), ex-boyfriend(이전의 남자친구)
5. save(절약하다), repair ≠ break down
6. broom (빗자루) → sweep (쓸다), sweep/swept/swept
7. love ≠ hate, everyone(단수취급), laundry(빨래)
8. 먼지 털고(dust), 바닥 청소(clean the floor), mop and bucket, nail and hammer, screw and screwdriver

Answer

01. graduated
02. divorced
03. bring
04. married
05. Fix
06. sweep
07. do
08. dust

※ 적절한 것을 골라 써넣으시오.

basement, husband, relatives, yard

01 Create your family tree and stay in contact with your ________.

02 Let's put it down in the ________.
We won't need it for several months.

03 Typically the goods in a ________ sale are unwanted items from the household.

04 Last week my ________, sister-in-law and I took a trip to Disney World.

1. family tree(가계), stay in contact with(와 접촉하며 지내다)
2. a floor below ground level
3. goods(물품; 상품), item(품목), unwanted(= unnecessary)
4. sister-in-law(남편 또는 부인의 sister), take a trip(= go on a trip)
5. stool(= backless chair 또는 feces)
6. chores to do
7. 수리가 아닌 것은?
8. 중퇴 또는 졸업이 아닌 것은?
9. 가격이 싸고 비싸고
10. upholstery(가구류; 좌석을 폭신하게 하는 재료)

※ 관계없는 하나의 단어에 X표 하시오.

05 shelf, stool, chair, couch, sofa

06 dust, sweep, vacuum, store, mop

07 repair, fix, break, mend, put right

08 leave, graduate, enter, drop out of

09 cheap, reasonable, costly, generous

10 sofa, rug, couch, club chair, love seat

Answer
01. relatives
02. basement
03. yard
04. husband
05. shelf
06. store
07. break
08. enter
09. generous
10. rug

1. during my absence (=while I am away), take care of(=look after; attend to) ≠ neglect
2. cheap/reasonable/expensive
3. cheap(=inexpensive), cancel(=call off), divorce (이혼)
4. quality(양질의), reasoning(이성적), cheap/inexpensive/reasonable/costly
5. a man or a woman
6. from head to foot, top down; bottom up
7. mop and bucket, screw and screwdriver
8. messy ≠ orderly
9. leave ≠ come back

※ 괄호에 적절한 것을 고르시오.

01 Will you (look, take) after my cat during my absence?

02 Are you looking for (cheap, expensive) but nice furniture?

03 It's cheaper to (call, put) off a wedding than it is to get a divorce.

04 Here you can buy quality furniture at a (reasoning, reasonable) price.

※ 반대 또는 대조되는 단어를 써넣으시오.

05 How **male** or **f**________ are you?

06 I cleaned the house from **top** to **b**________.

07 I rarely use **h**________ and **nails** as I typically prefer to use screws over nails.

08 I hate getting in a **messy bed** at night. So I **m**________ the bed before I go to sleep.

09 She **l**________, slept with some other guy, and is now trying to **come back** to me.

Answer

01. look
02. cheap
03. call
04. reasonable
05. female
06. bottom
07. hammer
08. make
09. left

※ 괄호에 적절한 단어를 고르시오.

01 Have you (divorced, separated) and then remarried the same person?

02 Do you (do, make) your fair share of chores around the house? Do you do dishes, laundry, vacuum, give your kids baths, change diapers, cook, do yard work etc.?

03 John was in the (base, basement), when his two dogs let him know something was wrong. "So I came upstairs and smelled smoke so I went all the way upstairs and this front room was not quite full of smoke but I could tell something was on fire." That's when he called 911.

04 Being the guardian and caretaker of your child, it is your responsibility to protect him/her from making such mistakes that are beyond repair. However, a lot of parents tend to be so protective of their children that they don't allow them to learn from their mistakes, which is a must. Give your child a safe and supportive home environment, along with the liberty to (make, correct) his/her mistakes.

1. 이혼했다가 다시 동일인과 결혼
2. do work; do housework; do chores, give a bath (목욕시키다), change diapers(기저귀 갈다)
3. basement(지하실), upstairs(위층으로), on fire(불붙은)
4. (토픽문장) 중간문장 allow them to learn from their mistakes. guardian (보호자), responsible → responsibility(책임) make/admit/hide/correct mistakes, beyond repair(고칠 수 없는), tend(경향이다), protective(보호하는), allow(=let; permit), a must(=necessity)

Answer
01. divorced
02. do
03. basement
04. correct

② Come and go

✵ fall/**fell**/fallen, tell/told/**told**, have told; was told, tell a lie/the truth, say/**said**/said, say something/yes, take/**took**/taken, take a picnic/shower/medicine, see/**saw**/seen, see a movie/doctor

우리는 한때 사랑에 빠져 애정 행각을 가진 적이 있다.

★ I **fell** in love with him.

★ I **was told** I looked like Zhang Ziyi.

He **said something** about his family.

★ We **took** a picnic at the beach.

We **saw a movie** last night.

✵ drive/**drove**/driven, mad(=very angry) lay/laid/**laid**, lay off(=fire), leave/**left**/left, come/**came**/come, hear/heard/heard pass/passed/passed drink/drank/drunk
※ passed와 past는 구분되지요? drunken은 형용사. celebrate → celebration (경축)

인생에 go down있으면, come up도 있게 마련

★ She sometimes **drove** me mad.

★ I was **laid off** due to budget cutbacks.

My first love **left** and never **came** back.

★ I hear he **has** just **passed** his exam.

★ We **have drunk** whisky in celebration.

그런데 laid, passed, drunk와 같은 과거분사는 도대체 어떻게 쓰이는가? 첫째, 과거분사는 완료시제에 쓰인다. 예를 들어 '2010년경 서울에 살았다'는 We **lived** in Seoul around 2010. 그런데 '2010년 이래로 서울에 살고 있다'는

✵ since(이래로), last year(작년에), for the last year(최근 1년간)

★ I **have lived** in Seoul since 2010.

이것은 'lived의 상태'를 '지금도 가지고 있으므로(have)' 과거와 현재에 걸쳐 있는 시제이다. 완료시제에 흔히 쓰이는 시간의 부사/부사구는 since, for the last week (최근 1주일), just, already, recently, lately 등.

둘째, 과거분사는 수동태에 쓰인다.

She **was seen** leaving the office.

★ She **was asked** to be with him forever.

※ (← They **saw** her leaving the office).
(← He **asked** her to be with him forever)

셋째, 과거분사는 형용사로도 쓰인다.

★ I was sweeping the **fallen** leaves.

Success is not for the **chosen** few.

※ 낙엽 (fallen leaves), fall/fell/fallen, 선택된 소수(chosen few), choose/chose/chosen, (사라진) He is **gone**. (주어진) **given** names, (도둑맞은) **stolen** money steal/stole/stolen.

시험과 관련하여 특히 유의해야 할 동사활용은 원형/과거형/과거분사가 모두 다른 경우이다.

(가다)	go/went/gone
(시작하다)	begin/began/begun
(먹다)	eat/ate/eaten
(마시다)	drink/drank/drunk
(운전하다)	drive/drove/driven
(타다)	ride/rode/ridden
(보다)	see/saw/seen
(선택하다)	choose/chose/chosen
(입다)	wear/wore/worn

원형/과거형/과거분사가 상이한 다른 예
lie/lay/lain
rise/rose/risen
write/wrote/written
speak/spoke/spoken
do/did/done
ring/rang/rung
draw/drew/drawn
grow/grew/grown
shake/shook/shaken
throw/threw/thrown
fly/flew/flown
break/broke/broken
steal/stole/stolen
hide/hid/hidden,
give/gave/given,
take/took/taken

※ 빈칸에 적절한 단어를 써 넣으시오.

1. 나는 예산감축 때문에 해고되었다.
2. 우리는 위스키를 마시며 경축했다
3. 나는 2010년 이래 서울에 살고 있다.
4. 그녀는 그와 영원히 함께 하자고 요청받았다.
5. 나는 장츠이처럼 생겼다고 들었다. And I resemble her still as an adult.
6. 우리는 바닷가에서 피크닉을 했다.
7. 나는 낙엽을 쓸고 있었다.
8. 나는 그와 사랑에 빠졌지.
9. 나는 CPA 시험을 통과했다.
10. 그녀는 때때로 나를 몰아 미치게 하였다.

01 I was **l**__________ off due to budget cutbacks.

02 We have **d**__________ whisky in celebration.

03 I have **l**__________ with my parents in Seoul since 2010.

04 She was **a**__________ to be with him forever. She said no.

05 As a teenager I was **t**__________ I looked like Zhang Ziyi.

06 We **t**__________ a picnic at the beach to enjoy the spring breeze.

07 I was sweeping the **f**__________ leaves of a tree outside our house.

08 I **f**__________ in love with him although he was two years younger.

09 He has **p**__________ his CPA exam. He's fortunate to pass it on the first try.

10 She sometimes **d**__________ me mad. When she promised we'd do something together I cancelled all my plans on that day and then she just said "Nah, I don't feel like going anymore."

Answer

01. laid
02. drunk
03. lived
04. asked
05. told
06. took
07. fallen
08. fell
09. passed
10. drove

※ 주어진 동사의 과거형을 써넣으시오.

Fred woke up around seven in the morning. After he **1.** get ________ up, he **2.** take ________ a shower. Then he had breakfast and **3.** read ________ the paper. Around eight fifteen he **4.** drive ________ to work. He started work at nine o'clock. At noon he had lunch in the cafeteria. At five thirty he **5.** finish ________ work. After work he **6.** eat ________ out with his friends. Then he **7.** return ________ home around eight thirty. Before he **8.** go ________ to bed he watched the news.

1. wake/woke/woken, get/got/gotten
2. take/took/taken
3. read/read/read
4. walk/run/drive to work, drive/drove/driven
5. finish work(일을 끝내다)
6. eat out(외식하다), eat/ate/eaten
7. return(= get back)
8. go/went/gone
9. in brief(= briefly), say yes/no/something
10. tell a lie/a tale/the truth
11. arrive ≠leave
12. give ≠take
13. child abuse(아동학대), see a movie/the doctor, watch TV/your step

※ 적절한 동사를 고르시오.

09 In brief they (said, told) "No."

10 Then he (said, told) the truth to me.

11 You arrived late, (leave, left) early. How rude!

12 You gave nothing and (take, took) everything!

13 I (saw, watched) some movies about child abuse.

Answer

01. got
02. took
03. read
04. drove
05. finished
06. ate
07. returned
08. went
09. said
10. told
11. left
12. took
13. saw

※ 적절한 동사를 골라 써넣으시오.

hear, listen, make, take

1. **listen to** music/the radio, **hear** the noise, often(= frequently)
2. **take** medicine/a walk, medicine(= medication)
3. I'm sorry? = Excuse me? say/said/said, pay/paid/paid
4. **make** a mistake, make a decision, make the bed(침대를 정돈하다)
5. a flight of(한 줄의)
6. resignation letter(사직서), give back(= return)
7. grow/grew/grown, throw/threw/thrown
8. accept(받다), application(지원서), begin/began/begun

01 How often do you __________ to music?

02 It's time to __________ your medicine, sir.

03 I'm sorry? I didn't __________ what you said.

04 We often __________ the mistake of leaving our bedroom window open.

※ 적절한 동사를 골라 과거형을 써넣으시오.

began, fall, read, throw

05 She __________ down a flight of stairs.

06 The boss __________ my resignation letter, and gave it back to me.

07 She was very upset. She __________ the saucepan at her husband.

08 The university __________ accepting applications in November.

Answer

01. listen
02. take
03. hear
04. make
05. fell
06. read
07. threw
08. began

※ have 아래에 적절한 과거분사를 고르시오.

01 Where have the flowers (went/gone)?

02 I have finally (passed/past) my exam.

03 I've (drunk/drunken) a bottle of Tequila.

04 I have never (ate/eaten) Italian food before.

05 Karen has (drove/driven) her truck for 6 hours and is very tired.

1. 사라지다
2. 통과하다
3. drink/drank/drunk
4. eat/ate/eaten
5. drive/drove/driven
6. do work,
   do a favor,
   do the laundry,
   do one's best
7. 해고하다 (fire; lay off)
8. take/took/taken
9. underpaid ≠ overpaid,
   live a life, make a living,
   miserable(비참한)
10. pharmacy(약국),
   침입하다(= break into),
   break/broke/broken

※ be 아래에 적절한 과거분사를 고르시오.

06 Why is your homework not (did/done)?

07 Was he (lay/laid) off because of his age?

08 Diego was (took/taken) by ambulance to the hospital.

09 They are (underpayed, underpaid) and live a miserable life.

10 The pharmacy was (broke/broken) into for the second time this month.

Answer

01. gone
02. passed
03. drunk
04. eaten
05. driven
06. done
07. laid
08. taken
09. underpaid
10. broken

※ 빈칸에 적절한 단어를 써넣으시오.

1. black out(깜깜해지다, 즉 기억이 하나도 나지 않다)
2. (토픽문장) 첫문장 Children should ~projects. encourage ≠ discourage, rely upon(=trust), convey(전달하다), have faith in(=believe in; trust), bring up(=raise), confident(자신감 있는)
3. (토픽문장) 끝 문장 The more ~ you love. unpleasant(=disagreeable), giving(베푸는 것), lead to(에 이르다), invite → invitation, offer(=give; volunteer), occasion(행사), the 비교급의 문장에 유의.

01 You black out because you drink too much too quickly. Drink much less and take your time to enjoy each drink if you want to **p**________ the blackout.

02 **Children** should always be encouraged and relied upon to take independent projects. For instance, if your child wants to clean the bedroom or make some craft, encourage him/her to go about it independently, without any support from you. This will convey to the child that you have faith in his/her abilities, which is the key to **b**________ up confident children.

03 Many years ago, I met a woman whom I found very unpleasant. So I decided to try out the "**giving** leads to love" theory. One day I invited her for dinner. A few days later I **offered** to help her with a personal problem. On another occasion I read something she'd written and offered feedback and praise. Today we have a warm relationship. The more you **g**________, the more you love.

Answer
01. prevent
02. bring
03. give

exercise 6

※ 동의어/반의어를 써넣으시오.

01 to make a choice = c__________

02 I was told about it. = h__________

03 to bring up children = r__________

04 to take care of health = l__________

05 to fix my broken chair = r__________

06 dirty clothes in the basket = l__________

07 a male student ≠ f__________

08 net income gain ≠ l__________

09 is encouraged to do ≠ d__________

10 They were overpaid. ≠ u__________

11 an inexpensive fridge ≠ c__________

1. 선택하다
2. 듣다
3. 양육하다
4. 돌보다
5. fix(= repair)
6. 빨래감
7. 남성의
8. 획득
9. 고무된
10. 과도하게 받은
11. expensive(= costly), fridge(= refrigerator, 냉장고)
12. spill(쏟다), spell(철자하다)
13. relate(관련하다), relative(친척)
14. do the chores
15. 졸업하다

※괄호에 적절한 것을 고르시오.

12 How do you (spill, spell) your name?

13 My favorite (relate, relative) was Ed.

14 I have many (chairs, chores) to do.

15 She (left, graduated) from school.

16. watch TV, see a movie
17. past week ;
    passed an exam
18. fall/fell/fallen
19. when getting
    → when they get,
    drink/drank/drunk
20. swear(서약하다),
    tell a lie/the truth,
    say something/hello

16 I (see, watch) a movie on weekends.

17 Then my aunt (passed, past) away.

18 My baby (fallen, fell) off the bed onto hardwood floor a minute ago.

19 They have (drunk, drunken) too much when getting behind the wheel.

20 Do you swear to (say, tell) the truth, the whole truth, and nothing but the truth?

My grade : ________/20

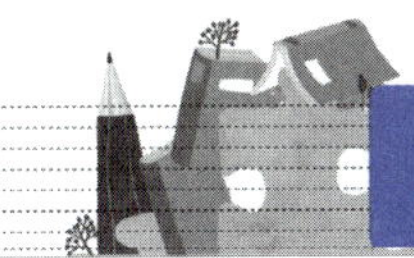

Test 6

ID :　　　　　　Name :

※ 주어진 단어를 사용하여 영어로 옮기시오.

01 저는 4명의 가족을 가지고 있어요. (have a family)

____

02 당신은 아침 내내 빨래를 했다. (all morning)

____

03 우리는 자녀를 엄격히 양육한다. (bring up, strictly)

____

04 나는 손자녀를 돌봤다. (look after)

____

05 그는 대학을 졸업했다. (a college)

____

06 나는 그와 사랑에 빠졌지. (fall in love with)

____

07 나는 예산감축 때문에 해고되었다. (lay off, budget cutbacks)

____

08 그녀는 그와 영원히 함께 하자고 요청받았다. (be with him)

____

09 우리는 위스키를 마시며 경축했다. (in celebration)

____

10 나는 2010년 이래 서울에 살고 있다. (since)

____

My grade : ________/10

Unit

07

Build your own garden

Unit.

07 Build your own garden

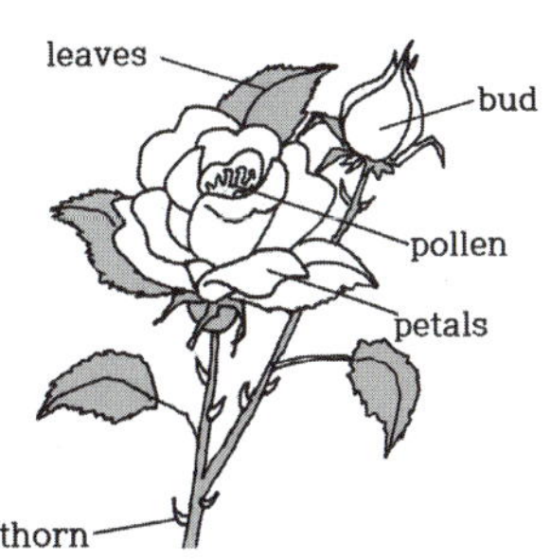

1 Grow vegetables

정원이 있는 집에는 거기에 나무를 심고, 채소를 가꾸거나 개를 기를 수 있다.

★ I **dig** a hole to **plant** trees or shrubs.

★ I **grow** vegetables in the garden.

★ He told me to **keep** a puppy.

※ dig/dug/dug, plant(식물; 심다), shrub(관목), grow(= raise), grow/grew/grown, vegetables(채소), keep(= **breed**), puppy(= young dog), keep/kept/kept

나무는 소나무(pine), 벚나무(cherry)이거나, 장미(rose)일 수도 있다.

★ The **pollen** of pine trees flies around.

★ We enjoy cherry **blossoms** in mid spring.

★ I have red **thorny** roses in the garden.

★ What trees **bloom** in early spring?

※ pollen(꽃가루), blossom(나무의 꽃), thorn(가시) → thorny, shade(그늘)→ shady, moss(이끼) → mossy, a mossy rock, bloom(= flower), early/mid/late spring

정원에서 기르는 채소 중에는 상추(lettuce), 토마토(tomato), 오이(cucumber), 배추 (cabbage) 등이 있다. 넓은 잔디밭(lawn) 조성도 가능. 그러나 잡초(weed)는 안 돼!

※ lettuce의 발음을 사전에서 확인!!
transplant(이식하다), seed(씨), seedling(= young plant grown from a seed, 모종), wither(시들다) ≠ prosper, mow(=cut), lawn(잔디; 잔디밭), rake(갈퀴; 갈퀴질하다), weed(잡초)→ weedy
weedy ≠ weed-free

★ You transplant lettuce **seedlings** into the garden.
What causes tomato plants to **wither** and **die**?

★ I mow the **lawn** every week.
I **rake** leaves off the lawn.

★ Make the lawn **weed-free**.

1. blow/blew/blown
2. creep/crept/crept
3. 파다
4. winds blow.
5. (톱)과 같은 철자
6. here와 다른 철자?
7. through와 다른 철자?
8. fallen leaves
9. brake와 다른 철자?
10. hit/hit/hit
11. the chosen few
12. lie(= be put)/lay/lain
13. lay(= put)/laid/laid

※ 원형/과거형/과거분사형을 써넣으시오.

#	원형	과거형	과거분사형
1	grow	grew	
2		kept	kept
3		dug	dug
4		blew	blown
5	see		seen
6		heard	heard
7	throw		thrown
8	fall	fell	
9		broke	broken
10	cut	cut	
11	choose	chose	
12		lay	lain
13		laid	laid

Answer
01. grown
02. keep
03. dig
04. blow
05. saw
06. hear
07. threw
08. fallen
09. break
10. cut
11. chosen
12. lie
13. lay

※ 빈칸에 적절한 단어를 써 넣으시오.

01 The **p**__________ of pine trees flies around.

02 I mow the **l**__________ of the front yard every week.

03 I dig a hole to **p**__________ trees or shrubs in the spring.

04 Get your grass healthy and make the lawn **weed-**__________.

05 He told me to **k**__________ a cute puppy, which I fell in love with right away.

06 Plant seeds indoors before you transplant **s**__________ into the garden.

07 I **g**__________ vegetables in the garden : garlic, spinach, tomato and green bean.

08 We enjoy cherry **b**__________ whose tiny petals are falling down like snowflakes.

09 What trees **b**__________ in early spring? If trees flower too early, a freeze could kill the blossoms.

10 I have red **t**__________ roses in the garden. Heavy-duty gloves are required for pruning overgrown rose bushes.

1. 소나무의 꽃가루가 흩날린다.
2. 나는 매주 잔디를 깎는다.
3. 나는 구덩이를 파서 나무나 관목을 심는다.
4. 잔디밭에 잡초를 없애요.
5. 그는 나에게 귀여운 강아지를 길러보라 했다.
6. 정원에 모종을 옮겨 심다.
7. 나는 정원에 채소를 기른다. spinach (시금치)
8. 우리는 벚꽃을 즐긴다.
9. 무슨 나무가 이른 봄에 꽃을 피우지요?
10. 나는 정원에 가시장미를 기른다. heavy-duty(튼튼한), prune(전지하다)

Answer

01. pollen
02. lawn
03. plant
04. weed-free
05. keep
06. seedlings
07. grow
08. blossoms
09. blooms
10. thorny

※ 적절한 동사를 골라 써넣으시오.

grow, keep, plant, water

01 They __________ peas on a very large scale.

02 How often should I __________ my vegetable garden?

03 The best time to __________ a tree is fall or early spring.

04 About one in 10 said their animal was too dangerous to __________.

1. 재배하다(= grow; raise), pea(완두콩)
2. often(=frequently), 물주다 (water)
3. Do not plant in late spring or summer.
4. 사육하다(= keep; raise; breed), dangerous(= risky)
5. forsythia(개나리), 꽃피다(bloom; flower)
6. difficult ≠ easy, transplant(=move)
7. pollen(꽃가루), blow/blew/blown, fly/flew/flown
8. official (공무원; 공식적), pest(해중), pesticide(살충제), residence(주거지) → residential, part → partial, essence → essential

※ 적절한 동사를 골라 써넣으시오.

blew, bloomed, spray, transplant

05 Forsythia, lilac and tulip have all __________ this spring.

06 Though never very difficult, it is not easy to __________ trees or move trees.

07 The pollen __________ around in clouds. And we suffered from horrible allergies.

08 Local government officials will __________ pesticide on residential trees on Monday.

Answer

01. grow
02. water
03. plant
04. keep
05. bloomed
06. transplant
07. blew
08. spray

※ 적절한 형용사를 골라 써넣으시오.

mossy, ripe, shady, thorny

01 The rocks were damp, __________ and slippery in places.

02 After harvest, __________ pecans are dried, sorted and graded.

03 It's the best to plant the tree in partially sunny to partially __________ locations.

04 Heavy leather gloves are essential when you cut down a number of __________ bushes in the backyard.

※ 관련 없는 하나의 단어에 X표 하시오.

05 dig, water, spray, plant, rake, lick

06 chimney, basement, yard, roof, floor

07 mow, polish, mop, sweep, dance, dust

08 ant, date, pansy, radish, lettuce, daisy

09 shoot, branch, trunk, twig, cork, car

1. damp(축축한), slippery(미끄러운), 이끼 (moss)
2. sort(분류하다), grade(등급지우다), 익은(= ripe; mature) ≠ (unripe; raw)
3. part/partial/partially, sunny ≠ shady, in the sun ≠ in the shade
4. essential(= necessary; required), bush(덤불)
5. gardening 관련. rake(갈퀴질하다)
6. building의 부분이 아닌 것? yard (마당)
7. chores가 아닌 것? dust(먼지 털다), sweep (쓸다), mop (걸레질하다)
8. plants 관련. date(대추야자; 날짜)
9. shoot(총 쏘다; 어린 가지), twig(잔가지)

Answer

01. mossy
02. ripe
03. shady
04. thorny
05. lick
06. yard
07. dance
08. ant
09. car

※ 괄호에 적절한 것을 고르시오.

1. 꽃봉오리
2. pet (애완동물)
3. the grass(=lawn, 잔디밭), mow(=cut), loan(대출)
4. bulb(구근; 전구)
5. sow(파종하다), harvest(수확하다)
6. keep a dog; grow vegetables
7. unsightly(보기흉한, unattractive)
8. flowers of a tree (=blossoms)
9. wither(시들다), cold(추위), drought (가뭄)

01 (Buzz, Buds) on the tree are a sign of spring.

02 Do you really want to (grow, keep) a cat as a pet?

03 The grass is wet. Is it OK to mow a wet (loan, lawn)?

04 You must (dig, fill) deeply in order to plant these bulbs.

05 Fall is the best time of year to (sow, harvest) your crops.

06 I didn't (grow, keep) any flowers this year, only vegetables.

07 (Weedy, Weed-free) grasses can give lawns an unsightly appearance.

08 The apple trees in spring are heavy with white and pink (flowers, blossoms).

09 The plants (wither, with) and die because of cold, darkness or drought.

Answer

01. Buds
02. keep
03. lawn
04. dig
05. harvest
06. grow
07. Weedy
08. blossoms
09. wither

※ 괄호에 적절한 단어를 고르시오.

01 Your seeds are now sprouting. They will need attention, just like (rising, raising) kids.

02 This insecticide will also kill spiders, fleas, ticks, ants and other household (fests, pests).

03 Some people say it's ok to (lake, rake) the leaves back in April from the flower beds, and others say it isn't! I can see the tulips coming up, but all my leaves from the fall are still in the beds. I am thinking to just move the leaves with my hands so as to be gentle with the (buzz, buds).

04 Sometimes I do spring clean-up just before weeding, raking fallen leaves out of the flower bed, cutting away old spent foliage, etc. What is important now, though, is to (move, remove) any weeds that have come up in the flower bed. If I can, I'll weed after a rain when the ground is (hard, soft) and yielding and the weeds pull up easily.

1. seed(씨), seedling(모종; 묘목), sprout(싹 트다), raise (=bring up, 양육하다), rise (일어서다)
2. insecticide(=pesticide), fest(축제), pest(해충)
3. leaf/leaves, wife/wives, wolf/wolves, some … others …
4. do cleanup, do laundry, do chores, weed(잡초제거하다), rake(갈퀴질하다), foliage(나무의 잎 전체), remove(=get rid of), yield(복종하다), yielding(순종하는), pull up(뽑히다)

Answer
01. raising
02. pests
03. rake, buds
04. remove, soft

② Dog and its puppies

✳ 임신(conception; gestation), dog and its **puppies**, cat and its **kittens**, bird and its **chicks**, sheep and its **lambs**, cow and its **calves**,

개는 63~65일의 임신 후 강아지를 낳는다. 고양이도 비슷하다(약 2개월). 새는 알을 품은 지 2~3주 정도면 새끼가 나온다.

★ A stray cat had 7 **kittens** in my garage.

★ These birds carried water for **chicks**.

✳ birds in the **nest**, spider on the **web**, worldwide web → www dog in the **kennel**, barn (외양간), stable(마구간; 안정적)

짐승(beasts)과 그들이 사는 장소도 함께 기억하자.

★ He removed the bird from its **nest**.

★ The spiders built a **web** on the ground.

★ Each **hive** had about 50,000 bees.

I plan on having a cow **barn**.

✳ wag(흔들다), bite(물다), scratch(할퀴다), creep(= crawl), chew(씹다), lick(핥다), as black as a crow as strong as an ox as quiet as a mouse as slow as a snail as deaf as a post as fast as light as heavy as lead

개개의 짐승이 갖는 특징도 함께 외우자.

Why does a dog **wag** its tail?

★ My dog tries to **bite** me.

★ My cat **scratched** me a minute ago.

Crocodiles **creep** around in muddy water.

★ I am **as blind as a bat**.

★ This load is **as light as a feather**.

✳ pet(애완동물), shelter(= refuge, 도피처, 보호구역), adopt(입양하다)

애완동물은 동물구호소에서 입양할 수도 있다.

★ You can **adopt** a pet from animal shelters.

※ 빈칸에 적절한 단어를 써 넣으시오.

01 This load was as light as a **f**__________.

02 About 50,000 bees live in each **h**__________.

03 I'm as blind as a **b**__________ without glasses.

04 These birds carried water for **c**__________ at the nest.

05 The spiders built a **w**__________ on the ground.

06 I found a stray cat who had seven **k**__________ in my garage.

07 My dog has always been friendly but he tries to **b**__________ me this morning.

08 My cat is one of the sweetest on the earth but he **s**__________ me a minute ago.

09 Please **a**__________ a pet from over 12,000 animal shelters across the country.

10 Do not remove the **n**__________ if an adult bird is resting inside because you might injure yourself or the bird.

1. 이 짐은 깃털만큼 가벼웠다.
2. 각 벌통은 약5만 마리의 벌을 가지고 있었다.
3. 나는 앞이 전혀 보이지 않아요.
4. 이들 새는 새끼에게 물을 날라주었다.
5. 그 거미들은 땅 위에 거미줄을 만들었다.
6. 떠도는 고양이는 새끼가 일곱이었다.
7. 내 개가 나를 물려고 한다.
8. 내 고양이가 조금 전에 나를 할퀴었어요.
9. 애완동물을 입양하세요. animal shelters(동물구호소)
10. 새의 둥지를 제거하다

Answer

01. feather
02. hive
03. bat
04. chicks
05. web
06. kittens
07. bite
08. scratched
09. adopt
10. nest

※ 적절한 동사를 골라 써넣으시오.

adopt, bite, crept, scratched

1. crocodile(악어), creep/crept/crept
2. scared(= frightened) bite/bit/bitten
3. puppy(= young dog)
4. indoor cat ≠ wild cat, vaccinate(접종하다), scratch(할퀴다)
5. light ≠ heavy, as heavy as lead
6. lose sight(시력을 잃다), have a very bad eyesight
7. careful(= wary), remove(= get rid of)
8. insect(곤충), crawl(= creep, 기다), get stuck(달라붙다), stick/stuck/stuck

01 Crocodiles __________ up and fishermen ran away.

02 My little sister was very scared. The dog tried to __________ her.

03 I want to __________ a husky puppy. Do you know where I can get one?

04 My baby got __________ by my indoor cat, who is vaccinated for everything.

※ 적절한 명사를 골라 써넣으시오.

bat, feather, hive, web

05 Your body feels as light as a __________ again.

06 The old man lost his sight. He is as blind as a __________.

07 Be very careful when you remove a bee __________ in the roof.

08 Insects fly or crawl into the __________ to get stuck. Then the spider eats them.

Answer

01. crept
02. bite
03. adopt
04. scratched
05. feather
06. bat
07. hive
08. web

※ 적절한 명사를 골라 써넣으시오.

chicks, kittens, lamb, puppy

01 Why does my cat lick her ________?

02 All the ________ have now left the nest.

03 How long does a sheep carry its ________ before delivery?

04 For obedience training we separate a ________ from its mother dog.

※ 관련 없는 하나의 단어에 X표 하시오.

05 bug, seedling, pest, insect

06 pet, nest, web, hive, kennel

07 ground, earth, worm, soil, dirt

08 chick, cow, kitten, lamb, puppy

09 fish, turtle, shark, puppy, hamster

10 ants, flies, fleas, lettuce, mosquitoes

11 swan, swallow, crow, bull, hawk, owl

1. lick(핥다), cat → kitten; kitty
2. nest (둥지)로 보아 birds or chicks
3. The average gestation period is around 110 days. delivery(배달; 출산)
4. obey(복종하다), obedience(복종), separate(분리시키다), separation(분리)
5. 해충이 아닌 것?
6. 집이 아닌 것?
7. 흙이나 땅이 아닌 것?
8. 새끼가 아닌 것?
9. 애완동물이 아닌 것? turtle(거북), shark(상어)
10. 해충이 아닌 것? flea(벼룩)
11. birds가 아닌 것? hawk(매), owl(올빼미)

Answer

01. kittens
02. chicks
03. lamb
04. puppy
05. seedling
06. pet
07. worm
08. cow
09. shark
10. lettuce
11. bull

※ 괄호에 적절한 것을 고르시오.

1. cattle(= cows and bulls), barn(창고; 외양간), stable(안정적; 마구간)
2. a dog house를 다른 말로 kennel
3. release(= set free), calm(차분하게 하다)
4. adopt(입양하다), 보호구역(shelter; refuge; sanctuary), slaughterhouse(도축장)
5. beat(구타하다), ex-owner(이전의 소유자),
6. lay eggs(알을 낳다), stuff(채워 넣다), leaf →leaves, life →lives, sign(간판)
7. dig/dug/dug, have dug, is dug, plenty of (= many; much), run off(발산하다)

01 My cattle are kept in the (barn, stable).

02 What size of kennel does my (cat, dog) need?

03 He released smoke into the (hive, heave) to calm the bees.

04 Adopt a homeless dog or cat from a local animal (shelter, slaughterhouse).

05 The dog was beaten by the ex/owner. He is (fond, fearful) of more beatings.

06 A bird nest is a place where a bird (lays, puts) its eggs. There are all kinds of nests, from cup nests to digging holes in the ground to simply stuffing some leaves inside the 'o' of a McDonald sign.

07 My puppy has (dug, digged) holes in my backyard. He lives inside. When I let him out to potty, he digs. They are all fun to him. He gets plenty of exercise. He even goes to puppy day camp to run off extra energy.

Answer

01. barn
02. dog
03. hive
04. shelter
05. fearful
06. lays
07. dug

※ 괄호에 적절한 것을 고르시오.

01 Lambs eventually grow into (ship, sheep).

02 Pull the (wiz, weeds) before you plant the flowers.

03 How long does it take to dig a grave with a (rake, shovel)?

04 Weed seeds will be (blew, blown) into a planting area by wind or dropped by birds.

05 My year old dog nips at my fingers, sleeves, etc. I am concerned that he will (bite, beat) my grandchildren.

06 Once the seeds start to grow they'll need 4 to 6 hours of light daily. For strong (seeds, seedlings) move them outdoors if the temperature permits.

07 We have a 4 year old cat that my hubby adopted from the shelter a few years ago for my Valentines Day gift. Today she (bit, scratched) my little boy right across the eye.

1. lamb(어린 양), eventually(=finally; at last)
2. wiz(=wizard, 마법사), weeds(잡초)
3. grave(무덤), rake(갈퀴), shovel(삽)
4. seed(씨; 종자), blow/blew/blown
5. year old(1년생), nip(=bite), concerned(=worried)
6. once(일단 ~하면), seed(씨; 종자), light(빛), daily(=every day), seedling(모종), temperature(기온)
7. adopt(입양하다), hubby(=husband), shelter(동물구호소), bite/bit/bitten

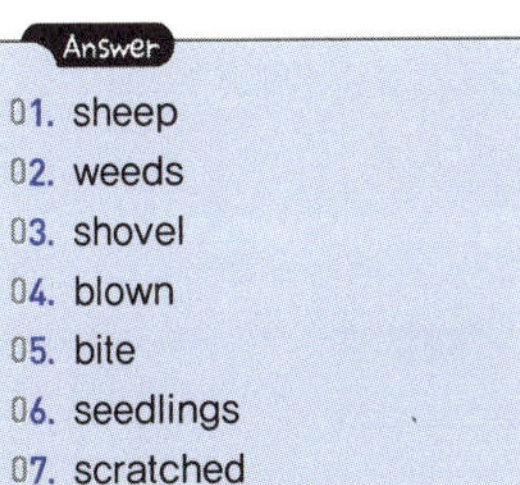
Answer
01. sheep
02. weeds
03. shovel
04. blown
05. bite
06. seedlings
07. scratched

※ 빈칸에 적절한 단어를 써넣으시오.

1. (토픽문장) Our host ~his hobby.
hesitate(망설이다),
odor(냄새),
orderly ≠ messy,
gorgeous(= very beautiful),
weary(= very tired),
guest ≠ host,
perennial(다년생),
annual(= yearly),
stroll(산책하다),
dense(빽빽한) → density,
float(떠있다)
2. (토픽문장) Whenever you ~ for incidents.
raise(= bring up),
prepared(= ready),
incident(사고),
inevitable = unavoidable,
get scratches(할퀴이다),
get nips(물리다),
nip(= bite lightly),
supervise(= oversee, 감독하다),
comfort(위안하다),
properly(절절히),
in the future/in the past/at present

01 We hesitated before we stepped into the garden, so heavy was the odor of flowering quince. The garden was orderly, comfortable, and gorgeous, with little benches artfully placed for the weary **g**__________. Our **host**, as generous as he was clever, introduced us to his hobby. We toured among hardy perennials, and walked past annual borders. We strolled among fig trees, past palms, to a density of shrubs. We floated in joy on the tropical air.

02 Whenever you raise your children along with pets, you should be prepared for incidents. These incidents are usually inevitable, especially if your children and your pet are playing. Children will usually get **scratches** from **k**__________ when they play. They may even get **nips** from **p**__________ if they are left unsupervised. Comfort your child whenever something like this happens, but you must also explain why the event happened. This way, your child can learn how to act properly in the future when around their pets.

Answer
01. guest
02. kittens, puppies

exercise 7

※ 적절한 동의어를 써넣으시오.

01	a young dog	= p________	1. 강아지
02	a young cat	= k________	2. kitty 또는?
03	a young plant	= s________	3. 모종
04	to keep horses	= b________	4. 사육하다
05	where bees live	= h________	5. 벌집
06	to nip my finger	= b________	6. 가볍게 깨물다
07	cherry blossoms	= f________	7. 꽃
08	to grow tomatoes	= r________	8. 재배하다
09	to mow the lawn	= g________	9. 잔디
10	find refuge in caves	= s________	10. 피난(처)
11	lawns full of weeds	= w________	11. 잡초 많은

12. seeds(씨), seedlings(묘목; 모종)
13. 사역동사(make), 꽃피다(bloom; flower), 시들다(wither)
14. grow vegetables, keep dogs, bring up children

※ 괄호에 적절한 것을 고르시오.

12 He scattered the (seeds, seedlings).

13 Rains made the yard (bloom, wither).

14 I (grow, keep) several tomato plants.

15. 깃털처럼 가벼운
16. crop(곡물)
17. bite(물다),
    scratch (할퀴다)
18. avoid(피하다),
    blow/blew/blown
19. not perfect → thorny
20. a few days old → chicks

15 Feel this bicycle. It is as (light, right) as a feather.

16 He has a farm, but chooses not to (plan, plant) any crops.

17 The kitten has just (bitten, scratched) the bottom of my left foot.

18 Pine (cone, pollen) is difficult to avoid and can be blown miles away.

19 Our life is like a (hairy, thorny) rose Not perfect, but always beautiful

20 The (chicks, chickens) in the nest are only a few days old and still blind.

My grade : ________/20

Test 7

ID :   Name :

※ 주어진 단어를 사용하여 영어로 옮기시오.

01 나는 구덩이를 파서 나무나 관목을 심는다. (trees or shrubs)

____

02 나는 정원에 채소를 재배한다. (grow)

____

03 그는 나에게 개를 길러보라 말했다. (keep)

____

04 소나무의 꽃가루가 흩날린다. (pollen, fly around)

____

05 나는 정원에 붉은 가시장미를 가지고 있다. (red thorny)

____

06 떠도는 고양이는 차고에 일곱 새끼를 가졌다. (a stray cat)

____

07 그는 새를 둥지에서 제거했다. (remove)

____

08 내 개가 나를 물려해요. (try to bite)

____

09 내 고양이가 조금 전에 나를 할퀴었어요. (scratch)

____

10 이 짐은 깃털만큼 가벼웠다. (this load, feather)

____

My grade : ________/10

Unit

08

Go on a picnic

Unit.

08 Go on a picnic

1 In your free time

여가 보내는 방법은 여러 가지다. 카드놀이, 음악, 뜨개질, 인터넷 검색, TV시청 등

We **played** cards together a few times.

★ She **performed** at family gatherings.

★ I learn to **knit** with hooks and needles.

★ I **surf** the internet on weekends.

They **watch TV** after dinner.

※ 여가 (leisure; free time),
play a musical instrument/ video games/cards
listen to music,
surf(파도 타다),
log in/out
watch TV/videos,
take pictures(사진을 촬영하다)

아니면 친구를 만나거나 쇼핑/관광, 동물원/ 박물관, 콘서트/영화, 술집/노래방, 클럽/춤 등

I **meet** with my friends over coffee.

★ I'll **do** some shopping downtown.

★ We **visit** the zoo and have a good time.

★ Dad allows me to **attend** a concert.

We often **see** horror **movies**.

★ We all **go to karaoke**.

※ meet/met/met,
meet(만나다; 충족시키다),
do gardening/ sightseeing/shopping,
go clubbing/dancing,
visit(= go and see),
attend(= go to)
see a movie,
horror movies(= scary films)
go to bars/karaoke,

※ jogging(= running),
good(= effective),
loss ≠ gain
play soccer/billiards,
play with jump ropes,
take a picnic/walk,
ride an escalator
drive a car

혹은 조깅/등산/축구/당구/줄넘기하거나, 자전거/말을 타거나, 피크닉/산보할 수도 있다.

★ **Jogging** is good for weight loss.

★ We **play** soccer, rain or shine.

Take a walk in the park with a friend.

★ I **ride** a bike for exercise.

(continued from page 72)

〈의문문의 유형〉

Yes/No Questions, Alternative Questions, Information Questions 등 다양한 형태의 의문문을 다시 한 번 연습해 봅시다.

1) "Have you finished your homework yet?" "**Yes**, I have."
2) "Would you like to go to China **or** Japan?" "Either place would be good."
3) "**Why** is Flight 474 delayed?" "There is a mechanical problem."

※ 빈칸에 적절한 단어를 써넣으시오.

1. "Is Tom working hard?" "Yes, he ________."
2. "________ did you get here?" "By subway."
3. "________ you read this book?" "Yes, I've read it twice."
4. "You can be there on time, can't you?" "No, I ________."
5. "You have never been to Paris, have you?" "Yes, I ________."
6. "How ________ have you lived in Seoul?" "For the last 5 years."
7. "________ position are you looking for?" "I hope to go into sales."
8. "________ organized the reception?" "Ms. Smith did."
9. "________ will the company hire more employees?" "Not until the end of the month."
10. "Would you like to look at the menu again _______ have you already decided?" "I'm ready to order."

Answers

1 is 2. How 3. Have 4. can't 5. have 6. long 7. What 8. Who 9. When 10. or

※ 빈칸에 적절한 단어를 써 넣으시오.

01 We **p**__________ soccer, rain or shine.

02 I'll **d**__________ some shopping downtown.

03 I **r**__________ a bike to lose weight and get in shape.

04 We all go to karaoke. What are your favorite **s**__________ to sing there?

05 Many people begin running because **j**__________ is good for weight loss.

06 My parents are not allowing me to **a**__________ concerts because they're 'rock.'

07 To make you scarves and gloves I learn to **k**__________ with hooks and needles.

08 We often **v**__________ the zoo. We rate it 4 stars out of 5 because we always have a good time there.

09 Throughout high school, she **p**__________ at talent shows and family gatherings, but she was never labeled a musician.

10 When I get home from work, I turn on my computer, wait until it boots up, and then go online to **s**__________ the internet.

1. 우리는 전천후로 축구한다.
2. 나는 도심에서 쇼핑을 좀 할 것이다.
3. 나는 자전거를 탑니다.
4. 우리 모두는 가라오케에 간다.
5. 조깅은 체중감소에 효과적이다.
6. 나의 부모는 내가 콘서트에 가는 것을 허락한다.
7. 나는 훅과 바늘을 가지고 뜨개질을 배웁니다.
8. 동물원을 방문하여 즐거운 시간을 가지세요.
9. 그녀는 가족모임에서 공연하였다.
10. 나는 인터넷검색을 합니다.

Answer

01. play
02. do
03. ride
04. songs
05. Jogging
06. attend
07. knit
08. visit
09. performed
10. surf

※ 동사를 골라 적절한 형태로 써넣으시오.

attend, go, ride, take

1. [be+ … ing/ … ed], ride a horse/a bike/ a cart/an escalator,
2. go hiking(= go for a hike)
3. spot(지점), take care/medicine / pictures
4. [have + …ed], arena(경기장), attend(= go to; take part in)
5. favorite song(애창곡), bar(술집)
6. fly(날리다), fun activity(재미있는 활동), windy(바람 많은)
7. play soccer/golf/ basketball, play the piano/violin/sax
8. bow (활)
9. do shopping/ sightseeing/ jogging

01 Some people are __________ the escalator.

02 Anybody can come on out and __________ for a hike with us.

03 This is one of the prettiest spots to __________ pictures in the fall.

04 More than 12,000 fans have __________ 2PM concert at the Olympic Park Arena.

※ 적절한 동사를 골라 써넣으시오.

do, fly, play, shoot, sing

05 What's your favorite song to __________?

06 I often __________ a kite on a windy day.

07 We are going to __________ basketball this weekend.

08 They like archery. They __________ at a target with a bow and arrow.

09 I __________ jogging everyday for 20 to 25 minutes. Is this too much?

Answer

01. riding
02. go
03. take
04. attended
05. sing
06. fly
07. play
08. shoot
09. do

※ be 아래에 현재분사를 만들어 써넣으시오.

handle, knit, surf, swim

01 She is now __________ a scarf using a crochet hook.

02 What happened to Gatsby while he was ________ in his pool?

03 How do I find out what websites my son has been __________?

04 Who is __________ its debt crisis better, United States or Europe?

1. [be+ … ing], hook/needle → 뜨개질하다
2. happen(=occur), pool(수영장)
3. find out(=discover), 인터넷 검색하다, log in; log out
4. debt crisis(부채 위기), 처리하다(=handle; deal with; cope with)
5. blow into the sax or play the sax
6. choose(=make a choice), watch videos/ see movies
7. go to(=attend)
8. 연기/연주/공연하다

※ 괄호에 적절한 단어를 고르시오.

05 Do you (blow, play) either the saxophone, trumpet or trombone?

06 Would you like to (see, watch) a movie at the cinema or a play at the theater?

07 Many people choose to (tend, attend) concerts to hear their favorite bands.

08 In addition to acting in the film, Brooke managed to write, record and (form, perform) 3 original songs in the movie.

Answer
01. knitting
02. swimming
03. surfing
04. handling
05. play
06. see
07. attend
08. perform

※ 취미의 명칭을 쓰시오.

1. tongs(집게), magnifier(확대경)
2. bow(활) quiver(화살통)
3. backpack(등산가방), compass(나침반)
4. tripod(삼각대), darkroom(암실)
5. plummet(낚시 추), bait(미끼)
6. music
7. pets
8. winter sports
9. outdoor sports
10. water sports
11. sports

01 **s**____________

album, tongs, magnifier, stamp

02 **a**____________

bow, arrow, quiver, target

03 **h**____________

map, tent, backpack, compass, hat

04 **p**____________

camera, flash, tripod, darkroom, film

05 **f**____________

rod, reel, line, hook, float, plummet, bait

※ 관련 없는 하나의 단어에 X표 하시오.

06 country/rock/film/jazz/classical

07 cat/mouse/dog/fish/parrot/worm

08 curling/skating/swimming/ice hockey

09 squash/ballooning/gliding/skydiving

10 diving/kayaking/rafting/sailing/chess

11 biking/circus/riding/archery/bowling

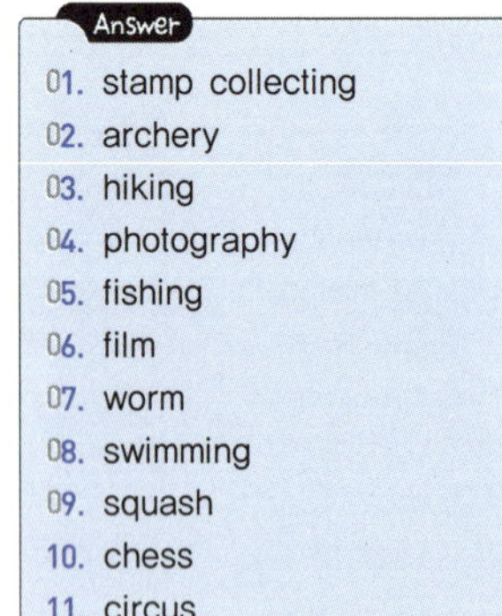

Answer

01. stamp collecting
02. archery
03. hiking
04. photography
05. fishing
06. film
07. worm
08. swimming
09. squash
10. chess
11. circus

② The stress relief

여가활동은 스트레스 해소에 도움이 된다. 먼저 영화, 경기관전, 여행 등을 통해 스트레스에서 벗어나자.

★ I am **moved to tears** by the film.

They're wildly **excited** over the game.

★ Are you traveling for **pleasure**?

※ stress relief, relief(= reduction), be moved to tears (감동받아 눈물 흘리다), excited(흥분된) for pleasure ≠ on business

다른 한편 스트레스의 출구(outlet)를 만들어주기 위해 지속적으로 움직이면 스트레스를 줄이고/격퇴하는 데 도움이 된다.

Why do boxers **jump rope**?

★ Many people join **a gym** to lose weight.

I go **hiking** in Palgong Mountains.

★ **Gardening** costs me very little money.

★ How can I **relieve** my stress?

※ 줄이다(relieve), 격퇴하다(combat), jump rope(= do jump rope; play with jump ropes), join(가입하다), go/do hiking, cost(~에게 ~의 비용 든다), relieve(= reduce; lessen)

좋아하는 것(favorites)을 즐기자. 노는 것 (play)은 재충전(refreshment)을 위해서도 필요하다.

★ I am very **fond of** Indian dishes.

★ She is **good at** all sports.

★ I'm **worried about** Dan. He can't swim.

★ Are you **satisfied with** your life?

★ Let's **celebrate** our victory.

※ fond/careful **of** ; good/excellent/ brilliant/superb **at** ; worried/concerned/anxious **about** ; satisfied/happy **with**, celebrate → celebration

※ 빈칸에 적절한 단어를 써 넣으시오.

1. 당신의 삶에 만족하세요.
2. 우리의 승리를 경축합시다.
3. 나는 그 영화에 감동 받아 눈물을 흘렸어요.
4. 그녀는 모든 스포츠를 잘해요.
5. 나는 인도음식을 좋아해요.
6. 체육관에 가입하여 체중을 줄이세요.
7. 나는 그것에 대해 걱정하고 있어.
8. 정원가꾸기는 나에게 거의 비용 들지 않아요.
9. 스트레스를 어떻게 완화할 수 있을까요?

01 Are you happy and satisfied **w**__________ your life?

02 Let's **c**__________ our victory over Manchester United!

03 I was **m**__________ to tears by the film titled 'The Road Home.'

04 She is good **a**__________ all sports. What sports are you interested in?

05 I am very **f**__________ of Indian dishes. My husband loves south Indian food a lot.

06 Please **j**__________ a gym to lose weight and reduce your chances of serious health conditions.

07 I go to a swimming club at school.
I just got my first period and I'm really worried **a**__________ it.

08 **G**__________ costs me very little money. I have spend very little growing vegetables and flowers in the garden.

09 I am constantly stressed in school and at home. I shout at my parents and my friends. How can I **r**__________ my stress?

Answer

01. with
02. celebrate
03. moved
04. at
05. fond
06. join
07. about
08. Gardening
09. relieve

※ 적절한 동사를 골라 써넣으시오.

celebrate, hiked, met, relieve

01 Has anyone here ever ________ the Black Hills?

02 She has ________ all graduation requirements.

03 You did it! Congratulations on your graduation. Let's ________.

04 Students got to ________ some stress and forget about the pressures of life by taking part in a pillow fight in Shanghai.

※ 적절한 것을 골라 써넣으시오.

business, crowd, gardening, gym

05 I've decided to join a ________ to get fit.

06 Traveling on ________ can be tiring and stressful.

07 He plays basketball and loves to hear the roar of the ________.

08 I love to grow veggies, fruit and flowers. I find ________ relaxing.

1. go up
2. grade(학년), graduate(졸업하다), graduation(졸업), 충족하다(satisfy; meet), meet/met/met
3. birthday/anniversary / graduation/ holidays to celebrate
4. stress → pressure of life, take part in(= participate in), pillow (베개)
5. want/decide/choose+(to 부정사), get fit(= get in shape)
6. business ≠ leisure/pleasure
7. play basketball, the crowd **roared**, roar(함성; 함성지르다), play the piano, the audience **clapped**, clap(박수; 박수하다)
8. grow(= raise), veggies(= vegetables), relaxing(긴장완화 시켜주는)

Answer

01. hiked
02. met
03. celebrate
04. relieve
05. gym
06. business
07. crowd
08. gardening

※ 괄호에 적절한 것을 고르시오.

01 She is very (like, fond) of animals.

02 He is (good, interested) at all sports that he plays.

03 Dad feels (happy, bad) with my grades in school.

04 They are old (sufficient, enough) to go skiing.

05 Why do people (wing, swing) their arms while walking?

※ 토픽에 해당하는 단어에 O표 하시오.

06 move/run/walk/stroll/skip/stride

07 water/plant/gardening/rake/shovel

08 mambo/rumba/samba/salsa/dance

09 cards/hobby/chess/pottery/knitting

10 soccer/skiing/hockey/sports/tennis

1. be fond of(= like)
2. excellent/good at.
3. satisfied/happy with; feel bad about
4. enough(= sufficiently)
5. move to and fro(= swing). while walking → while they walk.
6. stroll(산책하다). stride(활보하다)
7. rake(갈퀴로 긁다). shovel(삽질하다)
8. Latin dance
9. pottery(도예). knitting(뜨개질)
10. hawk(매). owl (올빼미)

Answer

01. fond
02. good
03. happy
04. enough
05. swing
06. move
07. gardening
08. dance
09. hobby
10. sports

※ 스포츠의 명칭을 쓰시오.

01 f__________

Yuna Kim/dancing on ice

02 i__________

goalie/mask/skate/puck/stick/ice

03 b__________

mound/outfielder/pitcher/shortstop

04 s__________

free kicks : indirect/direct/penalty

05 s__________

goggles/poles/snow/downhill/cross country

1. short program and free skating
2. Canada's national sport
3. Cubs, Yankees
4. goalkeeper
5. Pyongchang
6. ride a bike; drive a car
7. 사람이 아닌 것?
8. not a person? laughter(웃음)
9. amusements
10. make less 관련

※ 관계없는 하나의 단어에 X표 하시오.

06 horse, bike, cart, car, escalator

07 theater, conductor, performer, singer

08 actor, actress, cast, laughter, director

09 concert, musical, opera, comedy, ticket

10 raise, relieve, lessen, reduce, lower

Answer

01. figure skating
02. ice hockey
03. baseball
04. soccer
05. skiing
06. car
07. theater
08. laughter
09. ticket
10. raise

※ 빈칸에 적절한 단어를 써넣으시오.

1. 뜨개질하다
2. skinny jeans에 맞추려면 체중을 늘려? 줄여?
3. popular (대중의)
4. tragedy (비극)
5. in festive costumes (축제의상을 입은), dress up(차려입다), perform(공연하다), 연주(performance), 연주자(performer)
6. Austin's Sterling → the drug store, host(주최하다), throughout the store (매장 전체에)
7. (토픽문장) Accept the things you can't change. accept ≠refuse, unavoidable=inevitable, national recession (국가적 침체), cope with(=deal with; handle), as they are(있는 그대로)

01 I **k________** a flat scarf with **hooks and needles**.

02 I'm going to **l________** **weight** to fit into skinny jeans.

03 Which do you like better, **c________** music or **popular** music?

04 "Do you like **tragedy** or **c________**?"
"I prefer tragedy. It's deep."

05 **Performers** in festive costumes will invite the **a________** to join them in performing Christmas carols today.

06 Austin's Sterling will **c________** 60 years in business with an open house from 3 to 7 p.m. on Monday, Dec. 17. The drug store will host the community event by serving **free cake** and **giveaways**, along with **savings** throughout the store.

07 Accept the things you can't change. Some sources of stress are unavoidable. You can't prevent or **change** stressors such as the death of a loved one, a serious illness, or a national recession. In such cases, the best way to **c________** with stress is to accept things as they are.

Answer
01. knit
02. lose
03. classical
04. comedy
05. audience
06. celebrate
07. cope

exercise 8

※ 적절한 동의어를 써넣으시오.

01 to deal with it = h________

02 to go on a bike = r________

03 to get in shape = f________

04 I jog half an hour. = r________

05 to go and see her = v________

06 to go to the concert = a________

07 move through internet = s________

08 She is fond of jewelry. = l________

09 concerned about health = w________

10 become a member of it = j________

1. 처리하다
2. 타다
3. 건강한(healthy; fit)
4. 달리다
5. 방문하다
6. 참석하다
7. 탐색하다
8. 좋아하다
9. 걱정하는
10. 가입하다
11. bad/good/excellent/ brilliant at
12. knot(= tie, 매듭), knit(뜨개질하다)
13. garden(정원), gardening(정원 가꾸기)
14. do dancing/hiking
15. The story moved her to tears.

※ 괄호에 적절한 것을 고르시오.

11 He is good (at/in) ball games.

12 I started to (knot, knit) a scarf.

13 She said of (garden, gardening) skills.

14 We (did/made) some sightseeing today.

15 She was (mobile/moved) to tears several times.

16. 공연하다
17. 경축하다
18. please (기쁘게 하다) → pleasure
19. happy/satisfied with
20. 완화하다(= reduce; lessen; relieve), occasion(행사)

16 Broughton band will (form/perform) in Rose Bowl parade.

17 We are all awake at midnight to (celebrate, celebration) the New Year.

18 When somebody has thanked you, you say "It is my (please/pleasure)."

19 Only a few are satisfied (at/with) the direction the country is headed.

20 He attempted a couple of jokes to (leave/relieve) the tension of the occasion.

My grade : ______ /20

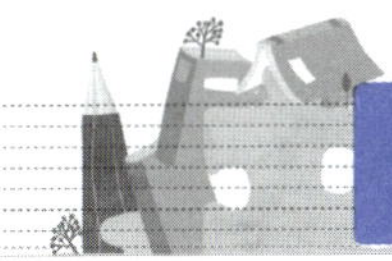

Test 8

ID :　　　　　　Name :

※ 주어진 단어를 사용하여 영어로 옮기시오.

01 그녀는 가족 모임에서 공연했다. (at family gatherings)

____

02 나는 도심에서 쇼핑을 좀 할 것이다. (some shopping)

____

03 아빠는 내가 콘서트에 가도록 허락한다. (allow, attend)

____

04 우리 모두는 가라오케에 간다. (go to karaoke)

____

05 우리는 전천후로 축구한다. (rain or shine)

____

06 당신은 여가여행 중이세요? (for pleasure)

____

07 그녀는 모든 스포츠를 잘해요. (good at)

____

08 나는 댄을 걱정해. 수영 못하잖아. (worried, Dan)

____

09 당신의 삶에 만족하세요? (satisfied)

____

10 우리의 승리를 경축합시다. (celebrate)

____

My grade : ________ /10

Unit

09

Snow fell heavily

Unit.

09 Snow fell heavily

1 The sun shone brightly

날씨(weather)는 일상생활에 영향을 준다. 해가 비치고, 바람이 불고, 비/눈이 내렸으면

★ The sun **shone** brightly on Friday.

★ The wind **blew** hard last night.

★ Rain has been **pouring down** all day.

★ The storm **lasted** 20 hours.

Snow **fell** fast and hard enough.

강풍(high wind; gust)은 호우(heavy rain; downpour)를 동반하여

★ The roads got **flooded** due to heavy rain.

★ The residents had to **evacuate** to safe areas.

★ It could take years to **recover from** the flood.

★ Heavy rain **forced** people to stay indoors in the morning.

✻ shine/shone/shone, blow/blew/blown, fall/fell/fallen
※ 단어를 욀 때, the sun **shines**, winds **blow**, snow **falls**, stars **twinkle**처럼 짧은 문장으로 외자.
it pours(= it rains heavily), it drizzles(= it rains lightly), all day ≠ all night, last(지속되다), fast and hard(= heavily)

✻ get flooded(침수되다)
heavy ≠ light, evacuate(대피하다), recover from (= get over; overcome), force(= impel; make)

※ affect(= influence),
life/lives,
wolf/wolves,
forecast(= predict),
cast/cast/cast,
forecast/forecast/forecast,
is forecast(= is likely)

따라서 일기예보는 매일의 중요한 관심사이다.

★ Weather can **affect** our daily lives.

★ A little snow is **forecast** for the area.

Snow is **likely** tonight.

1. 냉동식품(frozen food)
2. have risen
3. sunshine
4. lose weight
5. discover
6. 서있다.
7. ride a bike/escalator
8. have driven; is driven
9. have taken; is taken
10. have written; is written
11. hide and seek
12. cast/cast/cast
13. hit/hit/hit

Answer

01. frozen
02. risen
03. shine
04. lose
05. find
06. stand
07. ridden
08. driven
09. taken
10. written
11. hide
12. forecast
13. hurt

※ 원형/과거형/과거분사형을 써넣으시오.

#	원형	과거형	과거분사형
1	freeze	froze	
2	rise	rose	
3		shone	shone
4		lost	lost
5		found	found
6		stood	stood
7	ride	rode	
8	drive	drove	
9	take	took	
10	write	wrote	
11		hid	hidden
12		forecast	forecast
13		hurt	hurt

※ 빈칸에 적절한 단어를 써 넣으시오.

01 The wind **b**__________ so hard last night.

02 Heavy rain **f**__________ people to stay indoors in the morning.

03 The storm **l**__________ 20 hours for a total 1250mm of rain.

04 Rain has been **p**__________ down all night and all day where I am.

05 The sun **s**__________ brightly for an hour and then disappeared once again.

06 The residents should **e**__________ to safe areas until the storm passes.

07 It could take years to **r**__________ from the flood that has left millions homeless.

08 You can't get in or out of the city. The roads are **f**__________ due to heavy rain.

09 Weather can **a**__________ our daily lives in a number of ways from our mood to how we go about our day.

10 A little snow is **f**__________ for the area. The Weather Bureau sees a 30% chance of snow mainly before 11 a.m. Sunday.

1. 바람이 어젯밤 심 하게 불었다.
2. 호우로 사람들은 오전에 실내에 머물러야 했다.
3. 폭풍은 총1250mm의 강우량으로 20시간 지속되었다.
4. 밤낮으로 내내 비가 퍼붓고 있다.
5. 해가 밝게 비쳤다.
6. 주민들은 안전지역 으로 대피했다.
7. 홍수에서 회복하는데 수년이 걸릴 수 있다.
8. 도로가 폭우로 침수 되고 있다.
9. 날씨는 우리의 일상생활에 영향을 준다.
10. 다소의 눈이 예측된다.

Answer

01. blew
02. forced
03. lasted
04. pouring
05. shone
06. evacuate
07. recover
08. flooded
09. affect
10. forecast

※ 적절한 동사를 골라 써넣으시오.

affect, blows, falls, shines

01 The southeast wind __________ on the coast.

02 Let's go where the sun __________ brightly and the sea is blue.

03 The heavy snow could __________ holiday travel around Denver.

04 Snow __________ fast and hard over the weekend in the North Cascades.

※ 동사를 골라 적절한 형태로 써넣으시오.

blow, force, flood, raise

05 The high winds are __________ from colder areas.

06 The lake was rising rapidly and the road got completely __________.

07 Heavy rainfall has __________ the water levels in all major rivers and lakes.

08 People were __________ to spend most of their time in homes due to the snowfall.

1. snow **falls**; rain **pours**; winds **blow**
blow/blew/blown
2. the sun shines, stars twinkle, shine/shone/shone
3. affect(=influence, 영향주다)
4. fast and hard(=heavily), fall/fell/fallen
5. [be+ … ing/ … ed], high(=strong), winds blow, waves break,
6. [be/get + …ed], rise(=go up), covered with water(=flooded)
7. [have + … ed], water level(수위), 올리다(raise; increase), raise/raised/raised
8. [be + …ing/ …ed], 강요하다(=make; force; compel), were forced to (=had to)

Answer
01. blows
02. shines
03. affect
04. falls
05. blowing
06. flooded
07. raised
08. forced

※ 동사를 골라 적절한 형태로 써넣으시오.

evacuate, last, pour, recover

01 It has __________ with rain all day.

02 The heavy snow has __________ all week.

03 New Orleans is still __________ from Hurricane Katrina.

04 Residents were __________ from their homes by fire crews tonight

※ 동사를 골라 적절한 형태로 써넣으시오.

forecast, force, melt, rise

05 Snow is __________ and spring is on its way.

06 Heavy snow has __________ hundreds of schools to close across Britain.

07 Sea levels are currently __________ as water in the oceans is expanding.

08 More heavy rain is __________ over southern England for the next 24 hours.

1. [have + …ed],
all day → it pours,
It rains/drizzles/pours.
2. [have + …ed],
지속되다(= continue; persist; last),
all day → last
3. [be+ …ing/ …ed],
recover from(= get over; overcome),
4. resident(주민),
by fire crews로 보아 수동태 [be + …ed],
evacuate (대피시키다)
5. [be+…ing/…ed],
freeze ≠ melt,
on its way(= coming)
6. [have+…ed],
강요 하다(= force; make)
7. [be+…ing/…ed],
sea level(해수위),
currently(= now),
expand(= increase)
8. [be + …ing/…ed],
cast/cast/cast,
forecast(= predict),

Answer
01. poured
02. lasted
03. recovering
04. evacuated
05. melting
06. forced
07. rising
08. forecast

1. temperature
2. types of raining
3. types of winds
4. disaster 관련.
   avalanche(눈사태),
   landslide(산사태)
5. rainstorm 관련.
   a crash of thunder,
   a flash of lightning
6. go on(=run; last)
7. had to(must의 과거형),
   cancel(=call off),
   due to(=owing to;
   because of)
8. rise/rose/risen,
   (오르다) rise/rose/risen
   (올리다) raised/raised
9. likely(=probable)
10. affect(영향주다),
    effect(효과),
    on(날짜), in(달/연도)

※ 관계없는 하나의 단어에 X표 하시오.

01 wet, warm, hot, chilly, cold

02 rain, landslide, drizzle, pour

03 wind, breeze, gale, season, gust

04 flood, drought, forecast, avalanche

05 clear, thunder, lightning, crash, flash

※ 괄호에 적절한 것을 고르시오.

06 A winter storm can (go/last) for several days.

07 We had to (call, turn) off the game due to the bad weather.

08 The river's water level (raised/rose) to 6.7 feet this afternoon.

09 Heavy rain is (like, likely) to hit New Jersey and cause more flooding.

10 Heavy rain (affects, effects) parts of the North Island on December 17.

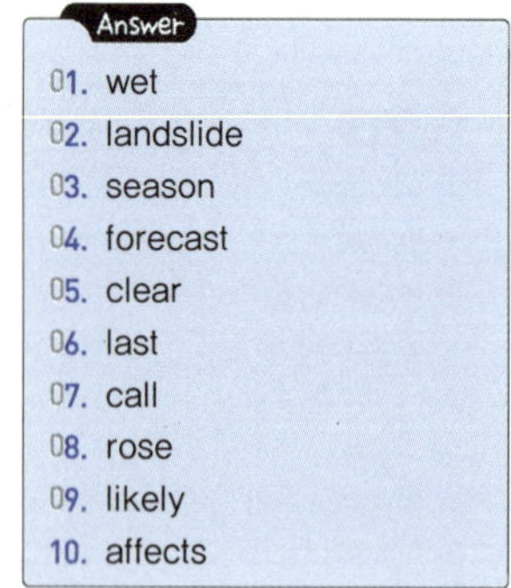

Answer

01. wet
02. landslide
03. season
04. forecast
05. clear
06. last
07. call
08. rose
09. likely
10. affects

※ 빈칸에 적절한 단어를 써넣으시오.

01 1. Why do people on the **g**__________ need to be concerned about ozone levels in the **air**?

02 The lack of rain in the North is causing a **d**__________, but in the South the rainstorms are causing **floods**.

03 Partly **cloudy** sky, with shallow mist was seen in the morning. It will be **c**__________ towards afternoon and evening.

04 If you have snow buildup on your rooftop, you might want to get rid of it before the **melting-f**__________ cycle begins.

05 I was involved in a car accident. I was driving out of my apt complex and used an exit that was fairly steep. The roads were **i**__________ but I thought that this road had been **salted**. As I drove onto the downward sloping road, I hit my brakes but it was too late.

1. concerned(= worried), in the air ≠ on the ground
2. lack(부족), lack of rain → drought, too much rain → flood(홍수)
3. mist(= light fog), cloudy ← partly cloudy ← clear
4. get rid of(= remove), melt ≠ freeze
5. involved in(연루된), steep(급경사의), icy ← salted

Answer

01. ground
02. drought
03. clear
04. freezing
05. icy

② On a wet windy day

✳ rain → rainy(= wet),
wind → windy, fog → foggy,
chill→ chilly,
used to (옛날에는 ~ 했다),
warm/hot/chilly/cold
명사) warmth/heat/ chill/cold
warm (덥히다), heat (데우다),
cool (식히다),
freeze (얼리다)

비/바람/안개의

★ What do you do on a **wet windy** day?

★ Winters used to be cold and **foggy**.

쌀쌀한 낮, 추운 밤. 몸을 덥혀주는 따뜻한 차!

★ Prepare for **chilly** days and **cold** nights.

★ **Warm** up with a hot cup of tea.

✳ frozen(얼은),
frozen food(냉동식품),
ice → icy,
icy road(결빙도로)

언 호수에서 낚시도 좋지만, 결빙도로 조심!!

★ I enjoy fishing on **frozen** lakes.

★ Be careful of the **icy** roads.

✳ hot → **heat**,
dry → **drought**,
dry spell(= drought),
hog(돼지),
barely(= just enough, 간신히),
hunger(= starvation),
malnutrition(영양실조)

여름은 더위(heat), 가뭄(drought; dry spell) 을 가져와 사람과 가축을 힘들게 하고,

★ The **heat** and the **drought** are so bad
that hogs can barely eat.

★ Millions of people suffer from **hunger** and malnutrition.

✳ breeze → breezy,
a breezy day,
shade → shady,
warm/warmer,
hot/hotter,
cool/cooler,
cold/colder

이런 때는 미풍(breeze)이 부는 그늘(shade)에 앉아서 쉬자.

★ Enjoy a cool **breeze** under a shady tree.

★ Ceiling **fans** make your house cooler

〈동사의 다양한 형태〉

1. 현재형	1) **He** travels a lot for work.
	2) **Many** (of them) travel overseas for business.
	cf) **Many** travels of Marco Polo
2. 과거형	He flew to China in 1994.
3. 조동사+동사원형	I had better ring him tomorrow.
4. have+…ed	I've always loved you since we kissed the first time.
5. be+…ing	Tom is taking a shower at the moment.
6. be+…ed	I am told to contact you immediately.
7. 동사구	What kind of music is listened to in italy?

※ 괄호에 적절한 것을 고르시오.

1. Jerry is always (lost, losing) his keys.
2. She sometimes (stay, stays) up all night.
3. Have you ever (drank, drunk) Fireball whisky?
4. You had better (take, taken) off your wet shoes.
5. We are (allowing, allowed) to bring our dog into the cafe.
6. I (must, had to) walk home last night. There were no buses.
7. The meat is coarsely (cut, chop) and seasoned with salt/pepper.
8. She (used, is used) to work in a shop. Now she works in a bank.

Answers

1. losing 2. stays 3. drunk 4. take 5. allowed 6. had to 7. cut 8. used

※ 빈칸에 적절한 단어를 써 넣으시오.

1. 쌀쌀한 낮과 추운 밤을 대비하세요.
2. 그늘 많은 고목 아래서 시원한 미풍을 즐겨요.
3. 나는 언 호수에서 낚시를 좋아해요.
4. 결빙 도로를 조심하세요.
5. 수백만의 사람은 굶주림과 영양실조를 겪고 있다.
6. 비오고 바람 부는 날에는 무엇을 하세요?
7. 옛날에는 겨울이 춥고 안개 많았다.
8. 천장 선풍기는 집을 한층 시원하게 해준다.
9. 올 더위와 가뭄은 참 심하다.
10. 나는 차를 마시며 몸을 덥힌다.

01 Prepare for **c**__________ days and cold nights.

02 Enjoy a cool **b**__________ under an old shady tree.

03 I go ice fishing every winter. I like fishing on **f**__________ lakes.

04 Motorists are reminded to be careful of the **i**__________ roads these winter days.

05 Millions of people in the world suffer from **h**__________ and malnutrition.

06 "What do you do on a **w**__________ windy day?" "I stay inside and take naps."

07 Winters in Milan used to be cold and **f**__________, but now fog is quite rare.

08 A ceiling **f**__________ makes your house cooler. Make sure it is turning clockwise.

09 The heat and the **d**__________ are so bad in this area that hogs can barely eat.

10 During the winter, nothing **w**__________ you up like a hot cup of coffee, chocolate, or tea.

Answer

01. chilly
02. breeze
03. frozen
04. icy
05. hunger
06. wet
07. foggy
08. frigid
09. drought
10. warm

※ -y로 끝나는 형용사를 만들어 써넣으시오.

01 chill ________ days of autumn

02 breeze sunny and ________

03 noise ________ kitchens

04 hunger ________ children

05 fog ________ harbors

06 star a ________ night

1. slightly cold
2. ease → easy,
   stone → stony,
   grease → greasy,
   rose → rosy,
   ice → icy
3. noise (소음)
4. starving(= very hungry)
5. fat → fatty,
   bag → baggy
6. Van Gogh's famous 'Starry Night'
7. look good(좋아 보이다)
8. risk(= danger, 위험),
   동파된(frozen and burst),
   burst/burst/burst,
   freeze/froze/frozen
9. Bermuda(카리브 해의 도서),
   offer(= give), mild(온화한)
10. stranger(낯선 사람),
    share(공유하다)

※ 적절한 형용사를 골라 써넣으시오.

frozen, mild, rainy, windy

07 How can I keep my hair looking good when it is very ________ outside?

08 Homeowners are at an increased risk of ________ and burst water pipes.

09 Bermuda offers ________ winter weather and plenty of leisure activities.

10 If a cute stranger asked you to share an umbrella on a ________ day, would you?

Answer

01. chilly
02. breezy
03. noisy
04. hungry
05. foggy
06. starry
07. windy
08. frozen
09. mild
10. rainy

※ 적절한 명사를 골라 써넣으시오.

breeze, fog, heat, spell

1. stay(= remain), cool(시원한), survive(~ 에서 생존하다)
2. cool(시원하게 하다)의 정도이므로 미풍(breeze) ≠gust; gale
3. drought(가뭄) → dry spell (건기), recall(기억나게 하다)
4. rarely(= hardly), in front of(= before), in back of(= behind), dense(= thick; heavy),
5. thunder(천둥), a crash of thunder, light(불 켜다), a flash of lightning
6. raise(= increase)
7. likely(= probable), covered in snow(= snowy)
8. humid(습윤한), hot and humid(고온다습한)

01 I want to stay cool and survive the summer __________.

02 There was a __________ on the beach, just enough to cool us.

03 Texas drought recalls long, punishing dry __________ of 1950's.

04 I could rarely see my hand in front of my face because of a dense __________.

※ 괄호에 적절한 단어를 고르시오.

05 Thunder usually follows (lighting, lightning).

06 The earth's temperature is raised by the (hot, heat) of the sun.

07 Your car is more likely to skid when the road is (icy, ice) or covered in snow.

08 Tomorrow the (weather, whether) will be hot and humid with the temperature above 40 degrees Celsius.

Answer

01. heat
02. breeze
03. spell
04. fog
05. lightning
06. heat
07. icy
08. weather

※ 토픽에 해당하는 단어에 O표 하시오.

01 hurricane/gust/wind/gale/breeze

02 season/fall/spring/summer/winter

03 warm/cold/chilly/frigid/temperature

04 rain/snow/storm/weather/sleet/cloud

05 flood/disaster/drought/typhoon/landslide

1. gust/gale(강풍)
2. 계절
3. lukewarm/warm/hot/chilly/cold/frigid
4. sleet(진눈깨비)
5. disaster(재앙; 재난)
6. hunger(굶주림)
7. Chili tastes hot.
8. dryness
9. spell(= period), hot spell(= heatwave), in the shade ≠ in the sun
10. keep warm; stay warm; feel warm, at least(최소한), little/less/least, once an hour(한 시간에 한 차례)

※ 괄호에 적절한 것을 고르시오.

06 We'll suffer from hunger but die from (thirst, thirsty).

07 I hope you brought your coat. It's a bit (chili, chilly) outside.

08 We had a (drought, flood) last summer. It didn't rain for six weeks.

09 There's a hot spell in June. They had to sit in the (shade, sun) every afternoon.

10 Keeping active will help you stay (warm, warmth). So try to move around at least once an hour.

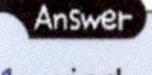

01. wind
02. season
03. temperature
04. weather
05. disaster
06. thirst
07. chilly
08. drought
09. shade
10. warm

※ 빈칸에 적절한 단어를 써넣으시오.

1. spring/fall→ season, preferred over (~보다 선호되는), northerly(북쪽의), latitude(위도)
2. (토픽문장) Most deserts ~ at night.
   dry ≠ moist,
   hold (=have),
   the sun sets
   ≠ the sun rises,
   considerably(상당히),
   clear(개인),
   release(=set free, 풀어놓다),
   at night ≠ in the daytime
3. land(육지),
   heat(더워지다),
   ground(지표),
   low pressure(저기압),
   hight pressure(고기압)

01 **Spring** and early **fall** are generally the best planting **s**__________ with spring preferred over fall in the more northerly latitudes.

02 The very **d**__________ air of the desert holds little **moisture** and thus holds little heat. As soon as the sun sets, the desert cools considerably. Clear, cloudless skies also help to quickly release heat at night. Most deserts have very low temperatures at night.

03 During the day land heats faster than water because water has a higher specific heat. Because the ground is warmer over land, the air is warmer over the land, low pressure develops over land. The water is cooler so the air above the water is cooler allowing for an area of high pressure to develop over water. Air always blows from high to low pressure so the **wind blows** from sea to land during the day. This is called a "sea **b**__________."

Answer
01. seasons
02. dry
03. breeze

exercise 9

※적절한 동의어를 써넣으시오.

01 a <u>wet</u> morning = r________

02 It is <u>rarely</u> used. = h________

03 <u>covered in snow</u> = s________

04 It will <u>rain heavily</u>. = p________

05 he <u>is forced to</u> stay. = m________

06 It was <u>a little foggy</u>. = m________

07 to <u>predict</u> heavy snow = f________

08 a <u>slightly cold</u> evening = c________

09 get <u>covered with water</u> = f________

10 to <u>get out of</u> buildings = e________

1. 비오는
2. 거의 않다
3. 눈 덮인
4. 호우 오다
5. 해야 한다
6. 옅게 안개 낀
7. 예측하다
8. 쌀쌀한
9. 침수된; 홍수 난
10. 대피하다
11. 냉동식품
12. make hot
13. calm (=quiet)
14. 건조한 (dry; droughty)
15. rain mixed with snow (= sleet)

※ 괄호에 적절한 것을 고르시오.

11 I don't eat (freezing, frozen) food.

12 (Hot, Heat) the water on the stove.

13 Calm weather won't (last, past) long.

14 Why is the air so (dry, drought) in autumn?

15 Rain mixed with snow is now (like, likely).

16. a bit(= a little),
be 동사 아래에 형용사
17. blow/blew/blown
18. recover from(= overcome)
19. affect(= influence, 영향주다), effect (효과)
20. The sun shone brightly.
I shined my shoes.

16 It's still a bit (breezy, breeze), but not as windy.

17 The wind (blew, blown) so hard it took everything with it.

18 The city will take time to (recover, overcome) from flood damage.

19 Heavy snow and ice will (affect, effect) roads across the highlands.

20 His face (shined, shone) like the sun. His clothes became as white as the light.

My grade : ________/20

Test 9

ID :   Name :

※ 주어진 단어를 사용하여 영어로 옮기시오.

01 폭풍우가 20시간 지속되었다. (last)

____

02 도로가 호우로 침수되었다. (due to heavy rain)

____

03 홍수에서 회복하는데 수년 걸릴 수 있다. (recover from)

____

04 다소의 눈이 예측되고 있다. (a little snow)

____

05 날씨는 우리의 일상생활에 영향을 줄 수 있다. (affect)

____

06 비오고 바람 부는 날에는 무엇을 하세요? (wet windy)

____

07 결빙도로를 조심하세요. (icy roads)

____

08 쌀쌀한 낮과 추운 밤을 대비하세요. (prepare for)

____

09 이번 더위와 가뭄은 참 심하다. (the heat, the drought)

____

10 수백만 명이 굶주림과 영양실조를 겪고 있다. (suffer from)

____

My grade : ________/10

Unit

10

Let me wait and see

Unit. 10 Let me wait and see

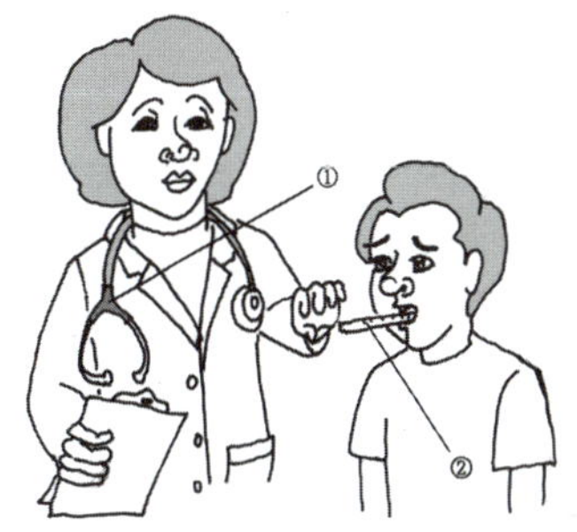

1 Lose weight

사람들은 체중을 '줄이다/늘리다/유지하다'에 관심이 많다. 일상생활에서 배설 관련의 표현도 꼭 필요하다.

★ Lose weight and **keep** it off.

★ I really need to **take** a pee now.

★ How often do you **open your bowels**?

★ Do you **sweat** too much?

※ (줄이다) **lose** weight, (늘리다) **gain** weight, (유지하다) **keep** weight
weight gain
weight loss,
take a pee/leak,
open/move bowels(= have bowels open),
sweat(= perspire)

통증 표현도 위급 사태에서 중요하다. 간단한 방법은 '아프다'란 hurt, ache를 쓰는 것이다.

★ My stomach **hurts**.

Why do my feet **ache**?

※ I **have a pain** in my stomach.
headache/ toothache/ backache/ earache/ stomachache

의사가 질병/환자를 치료하다/처방하다. 의사가 시키다(make)/충고하다(advise)/요청하다(ask)

The doctor **cures** heart disease.

★ He **treats** patients at children's hospital.

★ Doctors **prescribe** medicine and pharmacists fill **prescriptions**.

※ 치료하다(cure; treat), 처방하다(prescribe),

cure → **cure**
treat → **treatment** prescribe → **prescription**

fill(조제하다),
make(= force),
have(= get), let(= allow),

- The doctor forced me to lose …
- I got the nurse to check …
- Allow me to wait and see …

★ The doctor **made** me lose some weight.

[비교] The doctor **advised** me to lose …

★ I **had** the nurse check my blood sugar.

[비교] I **asked** the nurse to check …

★ **Let** me wait and see if he develops symptoms and then treat him.

〈동사구〉

동사는 전치사를 동반하여 목적어를 취할 수 있다. 예를 들어 believe in, agree to, deal with, look at 등이다.

※ 괄호에 적절한 전치사를 써 넣으시오.

1. This one belongs __________ me.
2. What do you look __________ in a job?
3. Can I count __________ you to do the job?
4. They believe __________ you and value you.
5. You should be ready to apply __________ jobs.
6. What kind of music is listened __________ in Italy?
7. It took years to recover __________ flood damage.
8. Do you have any difficulty dealing __________ stress?
9. Just a few women stay at home to look __________ kids.
10. Masked and armed thieves broke __________ the jewelry store.

Answers

1. to 2. for 3. on 4. in 5. for 6. to 7. from 8. with 9. after 10. into

※ 빈칸에 적절한 단어를 써 넣으시오.

01 Don't be hasty. **L**________ me wait and see.

02 I had the nurse **c**________ my blood sugar.

03 The doctor is a world famous specialist to **t**________ heart disease.

04 My stomach **h**________, but I don't have diarrhea, and I'm not hungry.

05 Doctors **p**________ medicine and pharmacists fill prescriptions.

06 We're not allowed to go during a test but I really need to take a **p**________ now.

07 Do you **s**________ too much? If so, find out what causes excessive perspiration.

08 "How often do you open your **b**________?"
"I have a big poop once or twice a day."

09 I went to a doctor who specialized in weight loss. The doctor **m**________ me do 45 minutes of exercise every day.

10 Lose weight and **k**________ it off.
A positive attitude is very important for successful weight management.

1. 기다려 봅시다.
2. 나는 간호사가 나의 혈당을 체크하도록 시켰다.
3. 그 의사는 심장병을 치료한다.
4. 배가 아파요.
5. 의사는 약을 처방한다
6. 나는 곧 오줌을 누어야 해.
7. 너무 많이 땀 흘리세요? perspiration(= sweating)
8. 얼마나 자주 대변을 보세요?
9. 의사는 매일 45분의 운동을 하도록 시켰다.
10. 체중을 줄이고 유지해요.

Answer

01. Let
02. check
03. treat
04. hurts
05. prescribe
06. pee
07. sweat
08. bowels
09. made
10. keep

※ 적절한 동사를 골라 써넣으시오.

flush, gain, open, treat

1. toilet(변기; 화장실)
2. underweight ≠ overweight
3. cure(= heal), colon(결장; 구두점의 콜론), lung(폐)
4. bowels(장), stools(대변), once/twice/three times difficulty(= trouble)
5. tummy(= stomach), 아프다(hurt; ache)
6. take medicine(복용하다), medicine(= medication), prescribe(처방하다), prescription(처방)
7. sweat(= perspire)
8. ICU(= intensive care unit), allow(= let)

01 Please __________ the toilet after its use.

02 An underweight person needs to __________ weight to be able to add muscle mass.

03 Avastin has been used to __________ colon, lung, kidney, and brain cancer.

04 I __________ my bowels less than 3 times a week, and have difficulty passing stools.

※ 적절한 동사를 골라 써넣으시오.

hurt, allowed, prescribed, sweat

05 Why does my tummy __________ after eating food?

06 He takes medicine __________ by a doctor.

07 You __________ a lot! People may assume you are unclean.

08 The hospital __________ patients recovering in ICUs to use iPads and communicate with nurses and family.

Answer

01. flush
02. gain
03. treat
04. open
05. hurt
06. prescribed
07. sweat
08. allowed

※ 괄호에 적절한 것을 고르시오.

01 I pour (sweat, wet) while performing shows.

02 Doctor, can you (force, make) me look like this?

03 They could only watch him (died, dying) of cancer.

04 I had my temperature (check, checked) by the nurse.

05 You don't have to (see, meet) a doctor for that fever.

06 I wish you the best of luck with your weight (lose, loss).

07 They learned to (deal, handle) any sort of emergency.

08 Why do I have my bowels (open, opened) in the morning?

09 I take a (pee, poop) in the morning.
It hurts when it comes out of my penis.

1. while performing(= while I perform), pour(쏟아 붇다)
2. look의 형태 유의. 사역동사 have(= get), let(= allow), make(= force)
3. 지각동사 see/watch/notice/hear/find/
4. 사역동사 have/make /let
5. fever(= temperature), consult a physician(= see a doctor)
6. to lose weight(= attain weight loss)
7. handle(= deal with), sort(= kind)
8. open(열린; 열다), 형용사(open)가 과거 분사에 우선
9. penis → 소변(pee), bowels → 대변(poop)

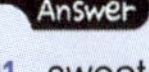

01. sweat
02. make
03. dying
04. checked
05. see
06. loss
07. handle
08. open
09. pee

※ 관계없는 하나의 단어에 X표 하시오.

1. 의료진
2. 질병
3. wig(가발), denture(틀니)
4. pill(= tablet)
5. toe(발가락), cheek(뺨)
6. cold(추운; 감기), catch a cold
7. take a leak; take a pee
8. ointment(연고)
9. palm(손바닥)
10. tooth decay(충치)
11. pediatrician(소아과 의사)
12. rash(성급한; 발진), athlete(운동선수), athlete's foot(무좀)

01 doctor, surgeon, physician, client

02 cold, warm, disease, illness, sickness

03 dentist, X-ray, wig, toothache, denture

04 pill, medicine, medication, operation

05 toe, cheek, lip, nose, mouth, eye

※ 토픽에 해당하는 단어에 O표 하시오.

06 cold/ulcer/flu/disease/diarrhea

07 pee/leak/urine/stool/sanitation

08 medicine/tablet/capsule/ointment

09 nail/palm/hand/joint/thumb/finger

10 crown/gum/tooth decay/dentistry

11 physician/surgeon/doctor/pediatrician

12 skin/rash/athlete's foot/burns/dermatitis

Answer

01. client
02. warm
03. wig
04. operation
05. toe
06. disease
07. sanitation
08. medicine
09. hand
10. dentistry
11. doctor
12. skin

※ 빈칸에 적절한 단어를 써넣으시오.

01 Dr. Teitelbaum **treated** hundreds of patients and refined his **t**__________ protocols.

02 Optometrists **prescribe** medications to treat certain eye diseases, and also issue spectacle and contact lens **p**__________ for corrective eyewear.

03 He still goes on walks and he will put his injured foot down when he lifts his leg to pee, and he will also lift the **injured** leg to pee. He is in no pain and he lets me feel around for an **i**__________, but I can't find anything.

04 Venezuelan President Hugo Chavez was undergoing surgery in Cuba on Tuesday for his recurrence of cancer, his friend and political ally Ecuadorean leader Rafael Correa said. "My dear friend and colleague, Commander Hugo Chavez, is going through the toughest times of his life," Correa said in Ecuador. "He's being **operated** on right now. It's a very delicate **o**__________."

1. refine(정교하게 하다), protocol(= manual)
2. optometrist(검안사), medication(= medicine), issue(발행하다), spectacle(= glasses), corrective(교정의),
3. injure(= hurt), lift(들어 올리다), pee(= take a leak)
4. undergo(= experience), surgery(= operation), recur(재발하다), recurrence(재발), ally(동맹국), colleague(= coworker), operate on (~를 수술하다), delicate(정교한)

Answer

01. treatment
02. prescriptions
03. injury
04. operation

② What is your stool like?

오줌/똥(**urine** and **feces**) 등의 안전한 처리를 위생이라고 한다. feces의 동의어로 stools가 있다. stool은 등받이 없는(backless) 의자, 변기, 똥의 3가지 뜻을 갖는다.

★ A **sanitation** worker was injured.

★ What is your **stool** like?

※ sanitation(위생; 분뇨처리) → sanitary, stools(= poop; feces), pee(= urine)
She sat beside him on the piano **stool**.
I unclog my toilet **stool**.
unclog (뚫다) ≠ clog

구강위생은 oral **hygiene** 또는 dental **hygiene**이라고 한다. 입안의 역겨운 냄새는 bad breath.

How do you practice good oral **hygiene**?

★ You have **bad breath** all the time.

※ oral(입의), dental(치아의), hygiene → hygienic, bad breath(입냄새; 구취), all the time(= always)

병명으로 두통/복통/암 등은 일일이 거론할 필요가 없겠지요. 자상 cuts, 타박상 bruises, 발진 rash, 화상 burns, 혹 lump 등은 관심을 가지고 연습해봅시다.

★ I'm okay; just a few **cuts** and **bruises**.

★ Mild **burns** can be treated at home.

※ 두통(headache)/복통(stomachache)/암(cancer), minor/mild(사소한), treat(= cure),

아프다고 전화하거나, 병가 중이면

★ She **called in sick** before the holidays.

★ Helen is **on sick leave**.

Let's **take a break** for a minute.

※ call in(전화 내다), write a sick note, on sick leave(병가중), leave (휴가), break (휴식), take a break(= stop)

병원에 가면, 간호사가 활력징후(vital signs)를 측정한다. 혈압(BP)/맥박(P)/호흡(R)/체온(T)

The nurse checked my **blood pressure**.

★ The nurse took my **temperature**.

※ BP(blood pressure), P(pulse), R(respiration), T(temperature), temperature(= fever)

질병에도 치명적/치료가능, 만성/급성

★ TB is a **deadly** but curable disease.

★ Diabetes is a **chronic** disease.

우리의 몸과 마음은 서로 연관되어 있어서,

Our **mental** health affects our **physical** health.

※ TB(tuberculosis), dead(죽은), deadly(= fatal, 치명적), 치료가능(curable), 치료불가능(incurable), diabetes(당뇨병), chronic ≠ acute,

※ body → bodily/physical mind → mental/psychic, emotion → emotional

〈형용사 + 전치사〉

동사뿐만 아니라 형용사도 곧바로 목적어를 취하거나, 또는 전치사를 동반하여 목적어를 가질 수 있다. 예를 들어 capable **of**, dependent **on**, doubtful **of**, familiar **with**, similar **to**, surprised **at**, grateful **for**, separated **from**, concerned **about**, interested **in** 등이다.

※ 괄호에 적절한 전치사를 써 넣으시오.

1. Are you good __________ singing?
2. Women are fond __________ jewelry.
3. You are responsible __________ your actions.
4. Are you familiar __________ Vietnamese food?
5. How do I tell a guy I am interested __________ him?
6. Fewer Americans are worried __________ food safety now.
7. What makes the movie different __________ the stage show?
8. I am harsh on myself. I am rarely satisfied __________ my own work.

Answers

1. at 2. of 3. for 4. with 5. in 6. about 7. from 8. with

※ 빈칸에 적절한 단어를 써 넣으시오.

1. 그녀는 휴일이전 에 아프다고 전화했다.
2. 그녀는 지금 병가중이다.
3. 좀 긁히고 멍든 것뿐이야.
4. 대변이 어떠했나요.
5. 결핵은 치명적이지만 치료 가능한 질병이다.
6. 간호사는 항문으로 나의 체온을 잰다. in my bottom(= rectally), 입으로?(= orally)
7. 넌 항상 입 냄새 나니?
8. 위생과 직원이 부상당했다.
9. 사소한 화상은 가정에서 치료될 수 있다
10. 당뇨는 만성병.

01 She called **i**__________ sick before the holidays.

02 She is on **s**__________ leave, not annual leave.

03 "Are your knees okay?" "Yeah, just a few cuts and **b**__________."

04 Talking about shit is often taboo… but what is your **s**__________ like?

05 TB is a **d**__________ but curable disease. If it is left untreated, TB can kill.

06 The nurse takes my **t**__________ in my bottom because it is mot accurate.

07 You have bad **b**__________ all the time. Just brushing and flossing isn't always enough.

08 A **s**__________ worker was injured as he was riding on the back of a garbage truck.

09 Everybody does something like sticking a finger to a hot pan now and again. Mild **b**__________ can be treated at home.

10 Diabetes is a **c**__________ disease. It is usually a lifelong disease in which there are high levels of sugar in the blood.

Answer

01. in
02. sick
03. bruises
04. stool
05. deadly
06. temperature
07. breath
08. sanitation
09. burns
10. chronic

※ 적절한 명사를 골라 써넣으시오.

bruises, burns, sanitation, temperature

01 Inadequate __________ is a major cause of disease world-wide.

02 My toddler is very active and always has ________ on his legs.

03 The nurse came back to check on me often and took my __________ rectally.

04 Most workers wounded in a factory fire on Friday suffered severe __________.

1. inadequate(= not enough), major ≠minor
2. toddle(아장아장 걷다), He has ever had a few **black eyes** too.
3. rectally ≠ orally, have a temperature (= have a fever),
4. wound(= hurt; injure), wounded → (who were) wounded, burns(= injuries caused by fire)
5. maternity (출산), pregnancy/maternity / parental/annual leave
6. normal ≠ abnormal, breath → breathe, bath → bathe, blood → bleed
7. wear(= put on), jog(= run), jogging → 땀(sweat)
8. loose ≠ hard, stools(= poop; feces), on and off(= occasionally)

※ 적절한 명사를 골라 써넣으시오.

breath, leave, stools, sweat

05 She took a month off for maternity __________.

06 It is normal to have bad __________ in the morning.

07 She wears a __________ band around her head during jogging.

08 I have had loose __________ on and off, mostly in the morning.

Answer
01. sanitation
02. bruises
03. temperature
04. burns
05. leave
06. breath
07. sweat
08. stools

※ 적절한 형용사를 골라 써넣으시오.

chronic, fatal, oral, sick

1. leukemia(백혈병), deadly(= fatal), curable(= treatable)
2. CKD(만성신장질환), get worse ≠ get better, worsen ≠ improve, over time → chronic, chronic(= deep-seated)
3. maintain(= keep), brushing (양치질), flossing(치실사용) → oral or dental
4. blood → bloody, water → watery, diarrhea (설사),
5. live → life, die → death
6. 내과의사/외과의사
7. It's nice and warm. The coffee is fine and strong.
8. 정신적(mental; psychic), closely(긴밀하게)
9. fever(= temperature)

01 Leukemia is __________ but curable.

02 __________ kidney disease slowly gets worse over time.

03 Maintain a regular __________ hygiene routine of brushing and flossing.

04 My friend once called in __________ saying that he had "bloody diarrhea".

※ 빈칸에 적절한 단어를 써넣으시오.

05 It's a matter of **life** and **d**__________.

06 **Physicians** and **s**__________ treat illness.

07 I'm **s**__________ and **tired** of traffic jams.

08 **M**__________, **emotional** and **physical** health and fitness are closely linked.

09 When you get a **t**__________, your body **rises above 98.6 degrees** Fahrenheit.

Answer
01. fatal
02. chronic
03. oral
04. sick
05. death
06. surgeons
07. sick
08. Mental
09. temperature

※ 반대 또는 대조되는 단어를 써넣으시오.

01 Exercising when you were **sick** … Is it **h**________?

02 My hands are **p**__________ and **numb** at night during sleep.

03 Anna Hazare who was **admitted** in the intensive care unit was **d**__________ on Monday.

04 How to **d**__________ a wound correctly is a good way to ensure that your cut doesn't get **infected**.

1. exercise(운동하다)
2. numb(무감각한)
3. admit(입원하다) ≠ discharge, intensive care unit(중환자실)
4. wound(상처), at night ≠ in the day time, ensure(= make sure), cut (자상)
5. lavatory(= toilet; restroom), laboratory(실험실)
6. prescription(처방), pharmacy(약국), phantom (유령)
7. reveal(= show), broken bones(= fractures)
8. dig(파다), drill(뚫다)
9. immediately(= right away)

※ 괄호에 적절한 단어를 고르시오.

05 A technician works in a (lavatory, laboratory).

06 Take this prescription to the (pharmacy, phantom).

07 The X-ray revealed that Sue had a broken (bone, born).

08 The dentist (digs, drills) through the tooth to get to the source of the pain.

09 He is very sick and should be taken to the (hospital, hospice) immediately.

Answer

01. healthy
02. painful
03. discharged
04. disinfect
05. laboratory
06. pharmacy
07. bone
08. drills
09. hospital

※ 빈칸에 적절한 단어를 써넣으시오.

1. resolution(결심), phrase(말하다), lose weight 하면, get in shape.
   fit(= in shape; healthy)
2. breathe(= take a breath), fill ≠ empty, lung(허파), inhale(= breathe in), exhale(= breathe out), reduce(= lessen), panic attack(공황발작)
3. last (지속되다), get better(= improve), on one's own(자력으로), serious ≠ light, fluids(= water), replace (대치하다), d______ → this common problem → the problem 에 유의.
4. sweat(= perspire), end up sweating(땀 흘리는 것으로 끝나다), bead(유리구슬), chin(턱), take a break(= take a rest), spill(쏟다)

01 Too many resolutions are phrased something like "I will **lose weight**", "I will get **f**__________" or "I will eat healthier."

02 To **c**__________ down, you need to breathe deeply, really filling your lungs. Inhale and exhale slowly. The act of taking in more oxygen will slow your heart rate and reduce the feeling of having a **panic** attack.

03 Anyone can get **d**__________. This common problem can last a day or two, or for months or years, depending on the cause. Most people get better on their own, but the problem can be serious for babies and older people if **lost fluids** are not replaced.

04 Every time there's a dance party, my face and head end up sweating like crazy. While dancing, beads of sweat drip off my nose and chin every few minutes. When I take a **b**__________ to go get a drink, people often remark on my sweat, asking whether someone spilled their drink on me.

Answer
01. fit
02. calm
03. diarrhea
04. break

exercise 10

※ 적절한 동의어를 써넣으시오.

01 to take a pee = l________

02 to shed weight = l________

03 My finger hurts. = a________

04 a deadly disease = f________

05 Allow him to go. = P________

06 a bodily handicap = p________

07 to have a big poop = s________

08 a treatable disorder = c________

09 You sweat too much. = p________

10 I have a temperature. = f________

11 a deep-seated disease = c________

12 injuries caused by fire = b________

1. urine; leak
2. 체중을 줄이다
3. 아프다
4. 치명적
5. 허락하다(= let)
6. 신체적인
7. feces
8. 치료 가능한
9. 땀 흘리다
10. 열
11. 만성적인
12. 화상
13. open/move bowels (= have bowels open)
14. write a sick note or call in sick

※ 괄호에 적절한 것을 고르시오.

13 I had my bowels (open, opened) today.

14 He (call, called) in sick on the most important day of the month.

15. my mouth stinks.
16. 사역동사 목적격보어 → 동사원형/과거분사, 지각동사의 목적격보어 → 동사원형/현재분사
17. 처방
18. leave of absence (=farewell)
19. treat(=cure), bumps(충돌; 혹), first aid(응급처치)
20. 사역동사(have/let/ make). 강제로 시키다 (force; make)

15 I brush my teeth constantly but I still have bad (breath, breathe).

16 They sit back and (let, see) everyone else doing the work.

17 The doctor gave her a (prescribe, prescription) for some medicine.

18 He took a (leave, leaving) of absence from the team for family reasons.

19 Treating bumps and (blues, bruises) is the most common type of first aid.

20 Angrily, mom (forced, made) my brother wash his face and brush his teeth.

My grade : ________/20

Test 10

ID :　　　　　　Name :

※ 주어진 단어를 사용하여 영어로 옮기시오.

01 나는 지금 정말로 오줌 누어야해. (take a pee)

____

02 얼마나 자주 대변을 보십니까? (open your bowels)

____

03 그는 아동병원에서 환자를 치료합니다. (treat)

____

04 의사는 처방하고, 약사는 조제합니다. (prescribe, fill)

____

05 의사는 나에게 체중을 다소 줄이게 시켰다. (make)

____

06 대변이 어떠했나요? (your stool)

____

07 그녀는 휴일이전에 아프다고 전화했다. (before the holidays)

____

08 헬렌은 지금 병가중이다. (sick leave)

____

09 결핵은 치명적이지만 치료 가능한 질병이다. (TB, curable)

____

10 간호사는 나의 체온을 재었다. (take)

____

My grade : ________/10

Answer Key

exercise 1

01 fly 02 reserve 03 board 04 claim 05 cancel 06 bag 07 postponed
08 Spanish 09 appear 10 recently 11 leave 12 bilingual 13 Russia 14 capital
15 languages 16 land 17 get 18 late 19 boarding 20 book

exercise 2

01 praise 02 give 03 unemployed 04 hobby 05 patient 06 host 07 nothing
08 strength 09 white 10 domestic 11 management 12 keep 13 promoted
14 do 15 laid 16 clients 17 critic 18 hire 19 application 20 recommend

exercise 3

01 trust 02 reliable 03 wicked 04 thankful 05 generous 06 talkative 07 calmed
08 orderly/organized 09 lie 10 unfriendly 11 doubt (distrust) 12 modest 13 found
14 grow 15 stand 16 wildly 17 interested 18 heard 19 patient 20 lie

exercise 4

01 slender 02 lose 03 floral 04 wear 05 fat 06 muscular 07 attractive
08 gorgeous 09 striped 10 youth 11 formal 12 resemble 13 straight 14 striped
15 weight 16 slim 17 loose 18 in 19 length 20 height

exercise 5

01 grind 02 consume 03 taste 04 uncooked 05 refreshments 06 drinks 07 heat
08 seafood 09 grill 10 worried 11 bowl 12 Grind 13 cook 14 bitter 15 with
16 Season 17 chop 18 recipe 19 bad 20 desserts

Answer Key

exercise 6

01 choose 02 heard 03 raise 04 look after 05 repair 06 laundry 07 female 08 loss 09 discouraged 10 underpaid 11 costly 12 met 13 relative 14 chores 15 graduated 16 see 17 passed 18 fell 19 drunk 20 tell

exercise 7

01 puppy 02 kitten 03 seedling 04 breed 05 hive 06 bite 07 flowers 08 raise 09 grass 10 shelter 11 weedy 12 seeds 13 bloom 14 grow 15 light 16 plant 17 scratched 18 pollen 19 thorny 20 chicks

exercise 8

01 handle 02 ride 03 fit 04 run 05 visit 06 attend 07 surf 08 likes 09 worried 10 join 11 at 12 knit 13 gardening 14 did 15 moved 16 perform 17 celebrate 18 pleasure 19 with 20 relieve

exercise 9

01 rainy 02 hardly 03 overcast 04 pour 05 must 06 misty 07 forecast 08 chilly 09 flooded 10 evacuate 11 frozen 12 Heat 13 last 14 dry 15 likely 16 breezy 17 blew 18 recover 19 affect 20 shone

exercise 10

01 leak 02 lose 03 aches 04 fatal 05 Permit 06 physical 07 stool 08 curable 09 perspire 10 fever 11 chronic 12 burns 13 open 14 called 15 breath 16 see 17 prescription 18 leave 19 bruises 20 made

Let me introduce myself

01 My name is ________________.

Hong Gildong, Kim Sunja

02 1) I'm **single** and live with my parents in ________________.

Seoul, Gumi, Chilgok, Seongju

2) I'm **married** and have a family of four: my husband(or wife), son, daughter and me. We live in ________________.

03 I'm going to graduate from ________________ ________________University/College.

04 I want to work as a ________________

nurse, social worker

here at the ________________.

hospital, nursing home, organization, company

05 I'm good at taking care of people, especially ________________.

children, the elderly, adolescents

I feel happy to help people in need.

1. (성명) Kim Sunja 또는 Sunja Kim
2. (가족) single(미혼의), married (결혼한)
3. (학력) 졸업하였으면 I graduated from …
4. (직무) 직업명 및 근무처. social worker(사회복지사), organization(기관)
5. (장점) be good at(~을 잘한다), take care of(= look after), the elderly(노인층), adolescents (청년), people in need(어려운 사람들)
6. (취미) most effective(매우 효과적), relieving stress (스트레스 해소)

06 I like ____________________

listening to music, hiking, soccer

because I find it most effective in relieving stress.

Thank you.

■ **김상한**

경북대학교 문학사, 문학석사

대구대학교 행정학박사

경북과학대학교 국제교육원장 역임

현 경북과학대학교 사회복지계열 부교수

〈주요 저서〉

김상한 외(관광통역안내, 경북 칠곡 : 경북과학대학, 2002)

김상한(Brushing Up My English, 경북 칠곡 : 보생출판사, 2008)

김상한(Communication in Nursing, 경북 칠곡 : 보생출판사, 2009)

김상한(My English improves, 서울 : 새벽숲, 2011)

김상한(practice makes perfect, 대구 : 도서출판 한영, 2012)

김상한(progress in my english, 대구 : 도서출판 한영, 2012)

Good at English

|저자| 김상한

|1판 1쇄 인쇄| 2013년 2월 10일

|1판 1쇄 발행| 2013년 2월 15일

|발행인| 김 동 훈

|발행처| 공 동 체

|주소| 경기도 고양시 일산동구 백석동 1323 동문타워 I 905호

|전화| 031) 920-8305(대표)

|팩스| 031) 920-8308

|e-mail| compub@naver.com

|출판등록| 2005년 10월 6일

|등록번호| 제396-2005-36호

|ISBN| 978-89-6352-456-6

정가 13,000원